The JANE FONDA WORKOUT BOOK

for Pregnancy, Birth and Recovery

by Femmy DeLyser

Photographs by Steve Schapiro

ADDITIONAL PHOTOGRAPHS BY HELLA HAMMID
DRAWINGS BY KATHY JACOBI

SIMON AND SCHUSTER · NEW YORK

LEFT TO RIGHT: *Femmy DeLyser, Laurie Venaglia with her three-week-old son, Brandon, Jane Fonda, and Jane Seymour Flynn, just before the birth of her daughter*

Acknowledgments

I am indebted to my students, too many of them to list here, for much of the content of this book. Their questions led me to further study in the field of childbirth, and to consult experts either in person or through their publications.

I am very grateful to the knowledgeable staff of the Obstetrical Department of Cedars-Sinai Medical Center in Los Angeles especially to Dr. Ian Ross Donald and Dr. Paul M. Fleiss and his assistant, Kittie Frantz, from whom I learned a great deal, and to Hospital Administration and the Departments of Medical Education and Child Guidance for their many years of hospitality extended to my work.

I thank Mary Kushner and others at Jane Fonda's Workout for their assistance with my program, and I thank especially Carol Gutierrez, Doreen Rivera and Jeanne Ernst for sharing with me their exceptional knowledge of exercise. The feedback from pregnancy exercise teachers Twyla Gonzalez, Jo-Ann Grossman, and Wendy Marsh was invaluable. So was the support of Ramelle Pulitzer and Jane Bello, and the patience of my typist, Anne Rice.

My friends, obstetrician Karen Blanchard and pediatrician Jeffrey Wasson, read the manuscript with great attention to detail. Their comments were a great help, as were those of Raul Artal, M.D., Professor of Obstetrics and Gynecology, and my conversations with Professor Barry S. Schifrin, both at the University of Southern California School of Medicine.

I thank Nan Talese for her invaluable encouragement and Fred Hills, Martha Cochrane, Leslie Ellen, and Eve Metz at Simon and Schuster for their concrete assistance. And finally I thank the Flinkman family and Chrys Atwood.

Copyright © 1982 by Femmy DeLyser and The Workout, Inc. All rights reserved, including the right of reproduction, in whole or in part in any form. Published by Simon and Schuster, a division of Gulf & Western Corporation. Simon & Schuster Building, Rockefeller Center, 1230 Avenue of the Americas, New York, New York 10020.
SIMON AND SCHUSTER and colophon are trademarks of Simon & Schuster.
Designed by Eve Metz.
Manufactured in the United States of America. Typeset by American Stratford Graphic Services, Inc., Brattleboro, Vt. Printed and bound by American Book–Stratford Press, Saddlebrook, N.J.

10 9 8 7 6 5 4 3 2 1

Library of Congress Cataloging in Publication Data
DeLyser, Femmy.
    The Jane Fonda workout book for pregnancy, birth, and recovery.

    Based on Jane Fonda's Workout program.
    Includes index.
    1. Pregnancy.   2. Exercise for women.   3. Childbirth.   4. Postnatal care.
5. Infants (Newborn)—Care and hygiene.   I. Fonda, Jane, date.   II. Schapiro, Steve.
III. Title.
RG558.7.D44   1982   618.2′4   82-10242
ISBN: 0-671-43219-2

The author thanks Tarzana Medical Center and Dr. Allen M. Entin for their cooperation, as well as those hospitals, doctors and nurses who did not express the desire to be identified.
Photo on page 20 courtesy of The Bettmann Archive, Inc.
Photos on pages 98 (top), 123, 129, 130, 133 (right), 136, 137, 139, 153, 155 (bottom), and 182 by Hella Hammid.

TO DYDIA AND ROLAND
AND TO HANS

Contents

Foreword

I first met Femmy DeLyser in her sun-drenched living room in Santa Monica, where I had come with my husband to begin a series of childbirth classes in preparation for the birth of my second child. Together with several other couples, we sat on the floor. Femmy gave the women large pillows to support their backs and bellies.

Femmy's voice, tinged with her soft Dutch accent, seemed to carry in its warmth a link to all women of all times who have shared this experience. She spoke to us not only of the profound changes our bodies were going through, but of the history of childbirth and how the customs surrounding it have changed through time and vary from culture to culture. She did not promise freedom from pain, but she explained that if we fully understood pregnancy, birth, and recovery, and learned the relaxation and breathing skills she would teach us, we would be better able to ride on top of the pain, not be submerged helplessly in it.

I had given birth to my first child five years earlier without such preparation, although I had very much wanted to experience natural childbirth. I had felt somehow that birthing would be a defining experience, one that would prove me to myself, but to hedge my bets I decided to try a teacher of the Lamaze method, which, it was implied, would make labor relatively painless. I was alone with her during the lessons, which consisted exclusively of breathing exercises. I found no comprehensive approach to childbirth, no support system and nothing about those little panting breaths that seemed likely to help me overcome pain. I gave up. As a result, when labor started, not only was I not equipped with a technique for handling the contractions, I was quite ignorant of what would be happening and I was overwhelmed by the pain—panicked. The doctor had wanted to conform to traditional rules—no husband in the delivery room—and I felt very alone in that unfamiliar, clinical environment. On top of that I had been heavily medicated and was unconscious when my daughter was born.

During my first pregnancy I had also been unhappy with my body. Accustomed though I was to regular and strenuous exercise, I had gone cold turkey for nine months out of fear of doing something to harm the fetus. I knew of nowhere to go for advice on how to continue a meaningful but safe exercise regimen while pregnant. Therefore, I did nothing. I grew puffier and more sluggish than I needed to be. I found myself confronting the greatest physical challenge of my life, feeling like a sack of overripe tomatoes.

I now know it needn't have been that way. Although Femmy had not yet developed the Pregnancy, Birth, and Recovery exercise program which is detailed in this book and which is now taught at my Workout Studios, my second pregnancy and delivery were quite different from my first. Femmy gave me a comprehensive understanding of the many changes my body was going through. I practiced the breathing exercises within a broad context of preparation and relaxation, and my husband was encouraged to learn along with me. When the contractions came and the birth was imminent I felt pain, to be sure, and at the final moment I asked for pain relief (the baby came before the local anesthetic took effect). But there was no loneliness, no panic. Femmy and Tom were with me, encouraging me, and in spite of the pain I still felt in control.

But again, during this pregnancy I had missed having a place to go or a book to read where I could be shown exercises suited to my needs as a pregnant woman. That is why, when I was about to open my first Workout Studio, I wanted to include a program of exercises for pregnant women, the kind of class I wish I'd had during my pregnancies. Frankly, I was thinking mainly in terms of exercises to maintain circulation and to

keep women from gaining too much weight. Because of the quality and depth of my experience with Femmy during the birth of my son, it was natural that I turned to her for help. And, as is her way, she said, "Why stop there? Why not design a total program of exercises and skills—not just for pregnancy, but for birth, recovery, and care of an infant?" And that's just what she did.

She knew that all women can learn the physical skills which will help them through the dramatic adjustments nature imposes on them before, during, and after birth. Women can strengthen the parts of their bodies where weakness may cause tension and pain: the legs, the lower back and the shoulder region. They can prepare for labor by improving body awareness, endurance and flexibility, as well as increasing muscle control in the pelvic region. Femmy would include in her program techniques for labor—for both the dilatation and the expulsion stages—as well as skills for receiving a newborn and nursing. But it didn't stop there.

Femmy wanted to get the new mother back into an exercise class as soon as possible, where she could do recovery exercises to help her regain posture, balance, strength and grace. And she wanted the moms to bring their babies with them. "The babies are as much a part of this class as they are a part of their mothers' lives," she said.

And so the Workout Studios opened, offering Femmy's Pregnancy, Birth and Recovery program—and a wonderful thing it has been to watch!

It did not surprise me that exercising helped the women who went through the program to feel better, gain less weight, recover faster, feel more energetic and become more aware of their bodies. What I had not anticipated was the value of the social interaction—the sharing. Though we don't always admit it, many of us are not at all certain how we will hold up in labor, how "brave" we'll be or how competent we'll be as new mothers. (What if I stick the baby with a pin? Roll on it in my sleep? Will it get spoiled if I come running every time it cries? Is the colic my fault? What's the best way to soothe it?) How wonderful to share these questions and fears! How great to learn, with a group of other new moms, how to relax your baby by massage. How special to share with others who feel—as you do—a little shaky, sometimes irritable, often joyous—in these first months of motherhood.

I had asked Femmy to put together an exercise program. Instead, she put together a whole little world that has made a profound difference, on

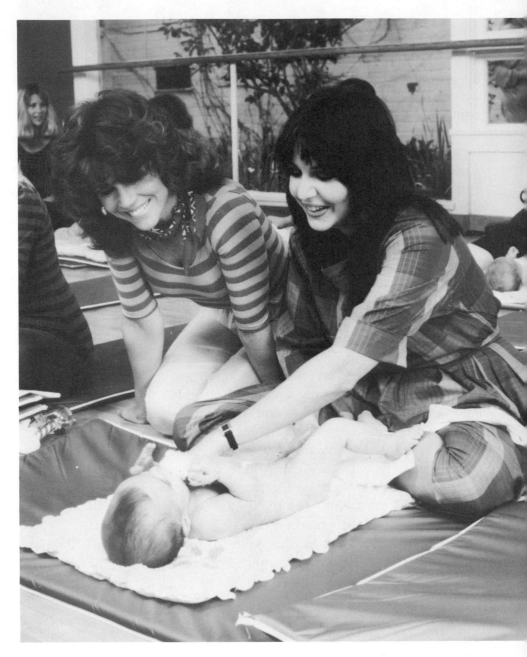

many levels, in the lives of its participants—the mothers, the babies, and always the fathers too. Her program is so special and so unique that I wanted pregnant women all over the world to be able to share in it—hence this book. Femmy has managed to bring her insights, humanity, feminism, medical knowledge and sensuality to every page on pregnancy, birth, recovery and parenting—that's the way she is. There's no book like it. She makes me want to do it all over again!

Jane Fonda

About the women and the pictures in this book

When I approached a Pregnancy Workout class of thirty women about modeling for this book, twelve showed a keen interest, and in subsequent months they gave much of their time and creativity to the project. They are, from left to right, Kim Holliday Norman, Abbie Scott, Sheryl Bernstein, Mary S. Byrum, Laurie Venaglia, Joyce Loo, Jo-Ann Grossman, Jane Seymour Flynn, Petronela Harris, Debbie Ormsbee Coltun and Kimberli Bronson Alame. One woman was absent when this picture was taken, Lindy Sanderson, who was in labor. She is the mother in Part Seven who demonstrates how to help a baby with cramps.

Besides their willingness to share their experience with others, the women had in common a commitment to exercise and the fact that they all expected their babies within a three-month period (Petronela Harris was due first and Jane Seymour Flynn last). Even though they all joined the Pregnancy Workout during their second trimester, we waited until everyone was at least six months pregnant before taking the photographs because before then a well-exercised body does not show much change in shape. The close-ups of the exercises were taken very near each woman's due date because it is then that pregnant women ask, "Should I still do this?" and "Am I doing this correctly?"—especially those at home without an instructor.

Nature appeared capricious as always, and some babies came early, some arrived late, some women had fast labors (Abbie's baby was born fifteen minutes after she arrived at the hospital, and Lindy and Sheryl, too, gave birth before the photographer arrived) and for others labor was long and arduous (Debbi's and Jo-Ann's lasted twenty-four hours). Two women—Petronela Harris and Laurie Venaglia—needed cesarean sections, both after laboring about twelve hours and after forceps were tried first. Our photographer, Steve Schapiro, was out of town when Jo-Ann Grossman's labor began, so those pictures were taken by Hella Hammid. The women shown exercising in the second trimester on page 27 are Rina Duchowney, Shirley Sherman, Linda Kagel and Rebecca Rothstein.

Not all hospitals allowed us to photograph and we were unable to record the delivery of Joyce Loo's baby in an alternative birth center without sterile drapes and stirrups and other medical paraphernalia.

We have selected from thousands of photos those that best illustrate the process of pregnancy, birth and recovery. The women wore leotards for the photographs—even for the preparation for birth and the early labor pictures—to enable the reader to see more clearly how the body is used. I am grateful to all these women for their generosity in sharing such an intensely personal experience. It was a pleasure to work with them, their partners, and with Steve Schapiro, who showed great sensitivity in taking the photographs for this book.

Introduction

A HISTORICAL
PERSPECTIVE ·

The first woman I saw in childbirth came from the red-light district in Amsterdam. She was one of five patients in the eight-bed communal labor and delivery room of an old county hospital and her labor was quite advanced. Her voice rasped over the moans of the others. Suddenly her defiant "Never again, not for me," changed into a frightened "It's coming out of my ass!"

"Push," said the nurse who was showing us nursing students how to take care of a woman in labor, while the doctor and his entourage—residents and medical students—grinned to each other at the woman's ignorance. They moved in closer now that the birth was imminent. Sweat dripped back into the woman's hair and her frightened eyes seemed to ask, "Why didn't anyone tell me?"

It was 1956. Birth preparation classes were new and the medical profession did not quite know what to do about them. As students of maternity nursing, we were required to know the content of both the Read and Lamaze schools. But both methods lacked intellectual sophistication and honesty; the skills they taught were helpful, but usually did not live up to their promise of a painless birth. The discrepancy between practicing in class and actually applying the skills during labor left many women fearful and feeling inadequate when the birth was more difficult than they had anticipated. Yet classes popped up like mushrooms and wherever they arose pregnant women rushed to take them.

In 1965, five years after I moved to California, I left the nursing profession to pursue a liberal arts education. I was awestruck at the variety of courses available. I thought of becoming an anthropologist. Yet at the same time, like many women approaching thirty, I wanted desperately to have a baby.

*Jane Fonda, nursing her son, Troy, for
the last time*

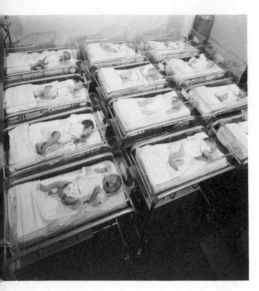

When I actually became pregnant, I wanted guidance and discovered an enormous void—the college did not offer a course on pregnancy, birth and recovery comparable in quality to its other courses. Birth preparation was still taught in someone's back room. Limited almost exclusively to breathing techniques for labor, these classes continued to pass on the misinformation and subjective opinions which had plagued them from the start. I did not want my husband or myself to waste time on methods which would only annoy both of us, so I decided against taking the existing courses. I was sure I knew how to handle labor from my training in maternity nursing and besides, I had heard that in America one could readily have pain-relieving medications.

But I did not know that in 1965 in an American hospital there was more to giving birth than coping with the process. Henry Ford's concept of the assembly line had affected maternity care. The mechanization of childbirth was in full swing and few women escaped the separation from their partners, the medication which while it deadened pain also altered their consciousness, the shot that numbed them from the waist down, the incision which widened their vaginas, the forceps which scooped out their babies, and afterwards, the lonesome recovery.

Babies were kept with their peers. A father admired his newborn through the nursery window, hoping that a kindhearted nurse would push its cot closer to the glass. Mothers could hold their newborns every four hours for twenty minutes. Parents and infant often did not meet as a family until the hospital nurse closed the car door for their trip home.

My husband trembled when he finally held his baby. As I watched him put her to bed, I realized with sadness how many lovely moments had been lost in the birth mill. Yet the birth had been easy and my baby and I were fine. How could I complain? I was afraid my doctor would reply with a brusque, "What did you expect?" I had what I wanted, yet something intangible had been lost in the process. I could not say what it was, nor could I put it out of my mind, especially during those first intimate weeks as I held my baby and watched her at my breast.

So many mothers I know have described with a special reverence their thoughts during nursing. As our eyes gazed at our babies and our breasts let go of the milk we sensed a common identity, a bond beyond and because of this individual experience. I thought often of all those other women—in ancient times, in other parts of the world, before hospitals and doctors and formal instructions. What were the conditions of their labors and how did they know what to do?

My mother gave birth to ten children on the river barge which provided our family with a livelihood. Barge people were sturdy and practical. Some still illiterate, they were a group unto themselves. To see a doctor because you were pregnant was an absurd notion. When my mother felt her time to be near, the boat stopped at a town on the river, and she would summon the local midwife who would come to the barge to investigate the living quarters and to give some final instructions. The last days of waiting began. If too much time passed, my father would begin to get impatient. "A boat has to move," he would mumble. But the barge remained tied to the pier.

When at last my mother's labor was well under way, my father would go to get the midwife. I remember at least three different ones, including one who spoke only German. My mother could not understand a word she said but the barge was on the Upper Rhine in the small town of Boppard and she had no choice. The midwife usually stayed on for an hour or so after my father had shown us our new baby. An aunt or a cousin who had come aboard earlier stayed to help with the household while the boat, after another few days at rest, resumed its course.

Had my mother been as surprised by the pain as the first woman I saw in labor?

"No," she said, "I knew what to expect. I had been with my older sister when she had her baby. She had learned from a cousin."

My mother did not understand or particularly like my growing desire to work on a formal birth instruction program. Her way of learning had been practical and sufficient. Plenty good enough for anyone, she thought. But she was fortunate because her labor was shorter and easier than that of the sister she had watched—what if she had observed an easy labor and then herself had been cursed with one that lasted two days? I hesitated to ask her that question. She spoke of her ease at handling births with such pride, and birthing and raising children had been her life. Because of that, I found after my daughter's birth that I could not discuss with my mother the nagging feeling of loss that had accompanied my own experience.

When I saw that the baby scooped from me was a girl, and how the natural perfection of her little life stood out in such stark contrast to the sterile environment of the delivery room, I, with my hands tied to the delivery table and my legs still in the stirrups, made my first promise as a mother. From now on nothing would be more important than helping this little being become who she was. If she was not to be locked in a prison of womanhood, I would have to break out of the invisible cocoon in which I still occasionally found myself trapped, a cocoon of dependence and subservience that was in part spun by my mother.

I had become, as I grew up, an enigma to my mother. Every step I took toward greater freedom and independence simultaneously threatened and liberated her. I could never tell her that it was in part the pain of her life which threatened mine, and spurred me on. I was determined not to become a woman whose life was spent washing and ironing and cooking and cleaning as she tended her children.

After I finished the elementary grades in a boarding school for barge children, I returned to the boat, but my desire for knowledge and an eagerness to join the real world made me search out a school in every town

Midwives with the tool of their trade—the birth stool—assisting a mother-to-be with the birth. Sixteenth-century woodcut by Martin Caldenbach

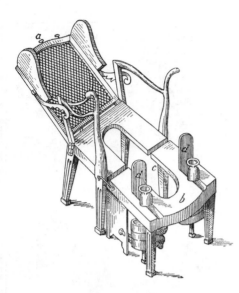

Note the improvement in the design of the birth chair. Designed by George Stein, eighteenth century

the barge stopped at to load or unload its cargo. A true education for me, a female, was even further beyond my parents' imagination than it was beyond their means, so I left their way of life when I was sixteen. Fourteen years later when I became a mother myself, the distance caused by time and experience and a different way of thinking left me with little to share with my mother. The invisible thread which each of us weaves toward individual growth tangles so easily. And I could not admit to my mother, who would not see that there might be a better way than hers, that I, who had rejected her ways, had lost something in the process.

While I did not confront my mother directly, I did carry on a dialogue with her in my mind as I pursued my new vocation as a birth educator. Learning about birth by witnessing, as my mother had done, may be useful, even beautiful, but it is not sufficient. Labor is unpredictable and variable. I knew that, despite the value of learning about childbirth by helping another woman through her labor, women needed to know much more about the experience, especially about complications and what to do should one occur.

There is in a woman's life no experience more exciting and frightening and momentous, I believe, than becoming a mother. To help her through this important time she should have the best instruction, not just for labor, but for pregnancy, recovery and infant care as well. And she should be able to make an informed choice about the setting for the birth, including hospital procedures. I decided to work on such a course. Since the information I needed was not available in a college or university, I became an obstetrical nurse again. I carefully selected a hospital where I could observe women in labor and the practice of American obstetrics. I also took the training provided by ASPO (The American Society for Psycho-Prophylaxis in Obstetrics), an organization started by Majorie Karmel and Elizabeth Bing to provide birth educators with some background. I studied the history of medicine and of birth practices, the physiology of labor, and the evolution of woman's consciousness. And I attended numerous seminars and workshops on obstetrics and maternity care as well as on exercise, yoga, massage and other health-related subjects. I began giving classes for expectant parents, and learned from them too about birth and after care.

My reading, this constant contact with health-care professionals and their clients, and my personal experience enabled me to formulate six observations on which to base my course:

1. A woman who exercises throughout her pregnancy feels and looks better while she is carrying her baby, and she recovers her figure faster after the baby is born.

2. A woman who has learned how to handle the pain of labor before it begins significantly improves her ability to endure.

3. Medicine is not practiced *on* a person but *with* a person. A treatment is much more likely to be successful when the patient is informed and consulted than when she is ignored and alienated. Her understanding of medical practices contributes to their success.

4. The relationships between health-care practitioners and their patients can develop the same problems as any human relationship, including those of dominance, of exploitation, and of blindness to the other's point of view. For those reasons, there must be dialogue. Standards of medical care improve with the quality of the communication, and the dialogue between obstetrician and expectant mother improves with birth education.

5. Preparation during pregnancy dignifies the father's role in the birth process. No longer barred from the scene, or a barely tolerated bystander, he becomes a skilled participant in the birth of his child.

6. Much of parenthood is said to be intuitive; however, this intuition can be helped with learning. Learning not just to handle labor but to adjust with good health habits to pregnancy, birth, recovery and infant care ahead of time gets a new family off to a much better start.

These six notions had shone through the distortions and limitations of the early childbirth education courses—one or more of these concepts helped each of the various classes to flourish. And the emergence of these concepts in childbirth education coincided with two scientific contributions to human reproduction: the ability to control conception and the ability to prevent excessive pain, injury or death during childbirth.

To realize how far we have come, consider for a moment circumstances in Europe during the Renaissance, when these new developments began. Until that time, birth practices had been remarkably similar from culture to culture and stable through time: women gave birth in an environment familiar to them. They were supported by other women, one of whom was usually a midwife. Midwives existed outside the medical profession, and they passed along their lore from generation to generation through an oral tradition of instruction. They learned primarily by apprenticeship, and many of them did not learn enough. In sixteenth-century England, the rediscovery of old Latin medical texts and their translation into English, combined with the earlier invention of the printing press, provided much valuable information for English women, some of whom brought these books to a friend's birth chamber to read aloud:

When man-midwives or physicians were first allowed to examine a woman in labor, they could touch but not see. In the interest of decency the room was darkened or, as in this seventeenth-century woodcut, the end of the bed sheet was pinned around his head.

The midwife must instruct and comfort the party, not only refreshing her with good meate and drinke, but also with sweet words, giving her hope of a good speedie deliverance, encouraging her to patience and tolerance, bidding her to hold in her breath as much as she may, also stroking gently with her hands her belly about the Navell, for that helpeth to depress the birth-downeward. But this must the midwife above all take heede of, that she compell not the woman to labour before the birth come forward and shew itselfe. For before that time all labour is in vaine, labour as much as yee list. And in this case many times it cometh to passe that the party hath labored so sore be-

A Coyotero Apache Indian method of assisting with a difficult birth. From George J. Engelmann's *Labor among Primitive Peoples*

fore the time, that when she should labour indeed, her might and strength is spent before in vaine, so that shee is not now able to helpe her selfe, and that is a perillous case.

These instructions were written for women who could not be helped by forceps or a cesarean section. A woman who could not push her baby out stood in danger of losing her life and her child's. Yet the publication of the second English edition of such a book of instructions for midwives had to be defended against public opinion. In the foreword the publisher says:

Some say it is unfit that such matters as these should bee published in a vulgar tongue for young heads to prie into. True but the danger being great and manifold, whether is it better that millions should perish for want of helpe and knowledge, or that such means, which though lawful in themselves, yet may by some be abused, should be had and used?

One sixteenth-century observer notes that women

in tyme of theyr travayle, moved through great payne and intollerable anguyshe, forswere and vowe them selfe never to companye with a man agayne; yet after the panges be passed, within a short whyle, for entyre love for theyr husbandes and singular delyte betwene man and woman, they forget both the sorrow passed and that is to come.

But once birth conditions improved through knowledge, women refused to go back to the old ways. With their persistence and the discipline of science, it took a mere four hundred years to loosen the complex and seemingly unbreakable bond between innocent pleasure and excruciating pain, until women could enjoy sex without worrying about conception, until they could have relief of painful labor, and until they could worry less about the incidence of injury and death during birth.

A curse had been lifted. Women were free. And in the intoxication of their new freedom they forgot that they might want to keep some part of the birth process. Obstetrics was a new medical science. And with the characteristic boldness of a new field it imposed its findings quite arbitrarily on a most ancient process. The resulting enthusiasm for controlling childbirth went a little too far; mechanization resulted.

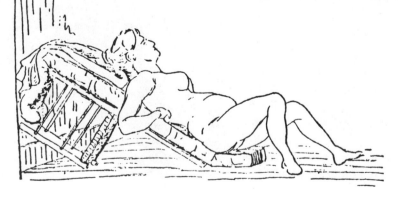

In search of a comfortable position for giving birth, French Canadians preferred to recline against a tipped-over chair covered with a mattress.

This standardization of a most natural process would not have been possible had it not coincided with a world view which saw control of nature as a desirable goal and accepted mechanization as an inevitable result. But errors of such magnitude cannot prevail very long. Nature reacted, showing us that our technology should be used with restraint; people rebelled, especially young mothers who felt dehumanized by sterile obstetrical techniques. The new childbirth practices began to be questioned, criticized and changed. Expectant parents began to search for sympathetic doctors who would cooperate with them in the process of birth. To meet their demands, birth preparation classes expanded and changed, and slowly childbirth is emerging from both the age-old cloaks of superstition and secrecy, and the new, dehumanizing technology.

Birth education need not interfere with the privacy of each expectant parent and it should not disregard people's personal modesty, nor their reverence for the process of birth. But it should provide people at a crucial junction in life with one of the most important disciplines of our species: education.

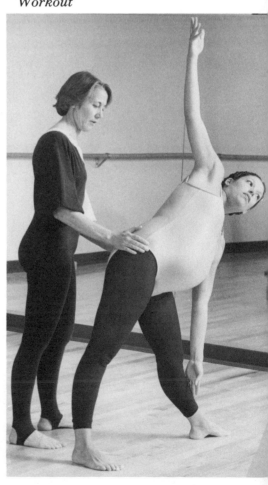

Femmy DeLyser teaching at The Workout

PREGNANCY, BIRTH AND RECOVERY: THE FOUR "TRIMESTERS"

Between conception and the time when a baby can go for a few hours without being held and fed lies a year of rapid physical change. A keen observer will notice seasonal changes within that year, each season lasting approximately three months except for one, the short but dramatic period of birth.

Since it is customary to divide pregnancy into three trimesters, it has been suggested that the first three months of the baby's life be called the "fourth trimester" of pregnancy, this to prepare the parents for the heavy demands of a new infant. Each trimester imposes on the mother its own demands, and if the parents interact closely the father too will feel the effects of this phenomenal experience.

THE FIRST TRIMESTER

During the first three months of pregnancy the mother's body tends to react strongly to her now high levels of estrogen and progesterone and to the suppression of the rhythmic release of ova. The physical symptoms vary, but many women are struck by the impact of the invisible pregnancy on their emotions as well. The new life within is in a very vulnerable period as it struggles to attain form. During this period, a woman should, without self-indulgence, listen to her body and not push herself to the point of exhaustion, perhaps to prove that nothing has changed. Good nutrition is as always crucial. But in these early months, it is more important to abstain from harmful substances than to eat great quantities of nutrient-packed foods. A body well-nourished before conception can, if nausea dictates, handle less food temporarily without harm to mother or baby. But the forming embryo is extremely sensitive to chemicals during the first trimester, even substances classified as food or beverages such as coffee and possibly even preservatives in foods. A woman should try to abstain from or at least cut down on drugs, alcohol, cigarettes and coffee during this period. For many women their nausea in the first three months forces them to forgo harmful substances, and is a blessing in disguise.

To counteract the nausea, pregnant women should try to eat foods rich in trace minerals—unrefined grains and a variety of fresh fruits and vegetables, preferably ones that have not been treated with chemicals. If she has the energy, the mother can exercise, but should do only the kind and amount the body is used to. Muscles change when they are worked intentionally and with sufficient repetition. Their structural change will in turn affect the overall metabolism. The details of how this affects the baby are still unknown but it is best not to expose the developing embryo to them until we know.

Extreme heat of sauna or hot tub should be avoided too, since the developing nervous system can be damaged by a great rise in the mother's temperature. If you do decide to have a sauna or hot tub, limit your time to fifteen minutes, since that is the length of time it takes for the inner-body temperature to rise. The heavy perspiration brought on by a sauna may also cause too great a biochemical upheaval.

Thus, a rule for the first trimester is: *make only those changes in living habits which the body dictates.* A woman who runs every day or one who is used to an exercise or dance program can continue if she feels up to it, but no one should commence a strenuous workout program immediately following conception.

THE SECOND TRIMESTER

Most women really enjoy the second trimester. Both mother and baby have made the initial adjustments. The pregnancy is well established and becomes visible without being in the way. The baby's movements become strong enough for the mother to feel. It has grown away from the lower pelvis and therefore causes less pressure on her bladder. Feelings of extreme fatigue generally disappear and there is usually little or no nausea.

A pregnant woman should not control her weight gain by a special diet, but by omitting foods high in calories and low in nutritional value. While she carries a child a woman should eat a well-balanced diet of wholesome proteins, unrefined grains and fresh fruits and vegetables. The amounts should be allowed to fluctuate from day to day and vary from woman to

woman. Metabolism is an individual matter and eating should not be regimented. Bodies react differently to pregnancy and such individual differences need to be respected. The biochemical and emotional stress which would result from repressing such differences is an unnecessary burden. A healthy weight gain during pregnancy ranges from fifteen up to as much as fifty pounds. The mother will often shed extra pounds without any effort during the recovery period, and if not she can lose them in the year following birth.

While all pregnant women expect to watch their bodies expand in the stomach and abdomen, they are often alarmed to see the almost equally common rounding of the arms and the shoulders, the hips and the thighs. Yet these fatty pads are probably the body's inevitable response to new hormone levels, like an exaggeration of the body's response to puberty. These fleshy areas usually disappear again during the year following birth. They seem to burn up with nursing, and they can be regarded more positively as a reserve, one of nature's ways of protecting her young sprouts from famine.

At the beginning of the fourth month, even a woman who was not used to working out would do well to strengthen her muscles, because in the six months to come they will carry a rapidly increasing load. However, she should not exercise on an empty stomach, because the muscles will burn up body fat for energy, and the by-products of that metabolism can be harmful to the baby. Exercise during pregnancy is not done for weight

control. A good time for a workout is a few hours after a meal but less than an hour after a wholesome snack, preferably one of carbohydrates such as whole wheat crackers, raisins or the like. Carbohydrates give the greatest and fastest energy with the least wear and tear on the metabolism.

In exercising, a woman should avoid strenuous work lying on her back, since in that position the full weight of her uterus rests on the large vein which returns the blood to the heart. This pressure, combined with the strain of exercise, can interfere with her circulation and especially with that of her baby. Long standing and heavy lifting are also not recommended; standing causes much more physical strain than moving, and the stress of lifting is often greatest in the lower abdomen and back, two areas burdened enough by the baby's weight, which increases daily.

Pregnant women should run only if they ran regularly before conception, and then only wearing well-cushioned shoes. Mothers-to-be should not run on concrete—the impact is too hard on the joints.

Walking is a very fine exercise, but not on thin-soled high-heeled shoes on city sidewalks. Flat shoes with a cushioned sole not only protect the joints, they encourage good posture. And only when the mother observes good posture does walking exercise the whole body without strain.

Swimming is probably even better than walking. Since the body is in a state of near weightlessness, there is less pressure on the circulation. With the blood flow thus unhindered, every muscle will be nourished while it is being worked and the waste products will be carried away.

A woman who rides horses, plays tennis or dances can continue until she feels hindered by her weight. I have seen women continue such activities well into the third trimester, without harm to themselves or their babies.

THE THIRD TRIMESTER

Toward the middle of the third trimester, many women find themselves wishing they could put the baby next to them for just a few minutes. The pregnancy is in the way—probably less so for a tall woman than for a short one, and less so for one who is physically fit than for one who is out of shape. But it is a difficult time for everyone. It is important to keep exercising though, not just to lessen the common discomforts of pregnancy, but to prepare the mind and body for labor.

LABOR AND BIRTH

Labor consists of two stages which require very different skills. During the dilatation stage when the uterus contracts and pulls the cervix open over the baby's head, the mother can allow this work to take place unhindered by practicing deep relaxation, especially between the waist and the knees. Such relaxation is helped by a fine muscle control. And muscle control is improved most easily by the proper exercise.

During the expulsion stage, the uterus contracts and pushes the baby through the now fully open cervix into the vagina which opens more easily—partly because of pregnancy hormone levels—thus allowing the baby to pass through. This stage requires skilled help from the mother. Her work can shorten the baby's journey through the birth passage and her muscle control at the moment of birth will safeguard the baby.

THE "FOURTH TRIMESTER"

Until birth, the infant moved as the mother moved, surrounded by the sounds of her body's workings. It sipped from the water in which it was submerged and drew nourishment continuously and without effort from its mother's body.

Now that the infant has experienced the dramatic separation of birth it will enjoy the new closeness when the mother puts it to her breast. The suckling of the infant releases oxytocin, the hormone which will simultaneously contract the uterus to help it return to its former size and location in the lower pelvis, and stimulate the glands in the breast to release colostrum, the special fluid produced to help the baby adjust to extrauterine life for the day or two before the milk comes in. A newborn infant likes to sleep in its mother's arms, its face nuzzled against her breast to take a sip or two whenever the urge arises.

During the first few days of recovery and new motherhood, there will be little time for reading or for learning new techniques. Therefore it helps for the mother to have learned beforehand how to take care of herself and the baby during those first days. She will feel more competent as she enters a new phase of womanhood, less helpless and nervous.

Many pregnant women don't bother to learn about the challenge of new motherhood because they believe it will all come naturally once the birth is over. But I think life is easy only when we give it our sincere effort and approach each new stage with knowledge and understanding, and this holds especially true for the initial phase of motherhood. A pregnant woman must also learn how to use such knowledge well. She will have to know about potential difficulties, but need not become insecure and fearful. Even if there seem to be a number of things that could go wrong, she should keep in mind that it is unlikely that any of them will. However, should she run into some sort of difficulty, she will know what to do.

A mother who has strengthened her arms, shoulders and upper back during pregnancy can hold and nurse her infant for longer periods without muscle fatigue and tension. An infant can pick up on its mother's tension without being able to release it, and become irritable.

As a new mother helps her baby find its own balance, she will slowly regain her former strength and grace. But first she too has to find a new balance and posture. Some of the techniques learned for the handling of labor—those of centering oneself and of letting go of tension—remain helpful, but they need to be supplemented with exercises designed for recovery.

Women who have just given birth often emerge from the experience with a special new reverence for life, something almost impossible to de-

scribe. Yet the amount of physical effort the process required remains very real. If woman could redesign her body, she would probably vote for special muscles to hold up her uterus in the last weeks of pregnancy, for an easy opening of her cervix and birth canal, and for an extra pair of arms to hold her baby close to her breasts those first three months after birth. But without those options she is likely to be eager for opportunities to share her experience and new feelings with the child's father, and to look to him for help.

A man's biological contribution to pregnancy ties him down for only an instant. After that he is free. His further contribution is one of choice, and to choose well must be quite difficult since his commitment relies almost entirely on the evolution of his consciousness. Society does prescribe a role for him, but the depth and extent to which he assumes his function remains much more a matter of choice than for a woman.

Perhaps the greatest change in man's approach to fatherhood has been brought about by the availability of birth control. Man too has been freed to reexamine his role as father. Many men now want to participate fully in the pregnancy and wish to be as closely involved in the birth process as possible.

The skills a man will need to learn for his initiation into fatherhood vary with his cultural background. In a tradition where the mother-child interaction is emphasized almost at the expense of that between father and child, it will be helpful for the father to learn how to handle an infant. I have found that when men do this they do it well, often with as much patience and less frustration than a woman. Many men find caring for and getting to know their infant quite special.

Men learn quite readily the techniques of supporting a woman in labor. The intimate knowledge lovers have of each other makes it possible for the man to better understand the woman's particular needs. During labor, as lover and father, he may be as emotionally involved as she is, even though he does not feel the physical pain. His special caring is a fundamental aspect of healing for the mother, an aspect often missing when all birth attendants are professionals. Often a woman will say that her labor was truly shared by her partner—"I could not have done it without him." For many men, the participation in their child's birth is an experience beyond words.

I was seven and had never left the barge overnight, when I learned about hospitals and nurses. Early one evening I was in the steering cabin watching a small town slip past. Because of the war the town was dark, but in one large building the lights were on and the blinds not yet closed. I could see women, all wearing similar clothes and caps, moving about in the rooms. Something about their movements appealed to me. I asked my father what it was.

"A hospital," he said. "Those are nurses, they care for the sick."

"I want to be a nurse," I said and both my parents believed it. Ten years later as a young nursing student, I wondered whether it was their saying "Femmy wants to be a nurse" or my desire to be one which accounted for my now wearing a starched apron and cap.

There, in that large county hospital in Amsterdam, I acquired two habits which kept me from being swept away by the immense current of human suffering: preparing my body for a heavy task with exercise, and handling pain with discipline.

Such a control of emotions starts with an overall disciplined approach to living, and the motivation and the rhythm of the discipline have to come from within. I believe we acquire this internal discipline in the face of hardship when the only choice is to do what needs to be done.

And while I don't want to make the challenges of pregnancy sound too severe, still the tasks ahead do inspire a woman to strengthen herself. Fortunately the strengthening of mind and body are not separate tasks. They go hand in hand. The repetitious movement of different body parts strengthens the muscles, and the discipline imposed by exercising regularly despite some discomfort strengthens the mind.

Part One

The Pregnancy Workout—
SKILLS & EXERCISES

GENERAL RULES FOR EXERCISING

Getting around to exercising in one's home is often more difficult than going to a studio. It helps to choose a particular time of day and a specific area in the house, and to make yourself exercise at that time each day. The workout area should have a mirror, something to hold on to (a doorknob or a solid handle in the wall) and an exercise pad.

Dress during a workout should not restrict the body and it should offer protection from cooling off too suddenly. Natural fibers breathe better and absorb perspiration, but they do not stretch like some of the synthetic materials. Leotards and tights made partially of cotton are a good choice, especially for a workout in a studio, since they allow the teacher a good view of how the body is being used. At home, if the temperature permits, you can exercise wearing no clothes at all. I don't believe wearing "just any old clothes" is a good idea. You should enjoy looking at yourself moving as gracefully as possible. Exercise to music with a good beat, songs you particularly like. Work out at least three times a week, and you will soon see improvements, especially if you do a few important exercises and stretches on a daily basis.

Most pregnant women—those who have not exercised in years as well as those who cannot live without a daily workout—look for a book with instructions for pregnancy exercises. And each woman should use such instructions according to her particular needs. For your own and your baby's safety observe the following rules:

- Discuss your intention to start the exercises in this book with your physician to make sure there are no medical objections. If you have a condition which necessitates that you stay off your feet, you can still practice the breathing and relaxation. If your doctor believes the one-hour program is too much for you, the daily warm-up exercises may still be fine.
- Before you start to exercise give the whole exercise chapter a quick reading and look at the pictures. Don't worry if the details seem overwhelming and don't try to remember them all. Reread the chapter with more attention to detail the next day, then try the exercises from the sections on posture, breathing and warm-up and those from the Pregnancy Workout marked with an asterisk. When those become a daily

routine for which you no longer need the book, begin to add the others on days when you have more time.

- Be realistic about the condition of your muscles. Do not start with a vengeance; begin instead with only a few repetitions of each exercise just to learn how to do each one correctly. Then increase the amount of repetitions daily.

- If a particular exercise hurts you every time you do it, check if you are doing it correctly. If you are, leave that exercise out. Bodies react very differently to pregnancy and none of the exercises should hurt.

- If your body is in good shape and exercising from a book is easy for you, enjoy your proficiency and start at your own pace.

- Let go of the idea that a specific trimester demands a particular exercise routine. It is the condition of your muscles and cardiovascular system that determines what you can do—not the number of weeks you have been pregnant. For the baby it is the quality of the placenta which determines how it gets along while you exercise. Your doctor can determine that by monitoring your baby's heartbeat.

- Realize that the body still has cycles, and days of abundant energy may be followed by days of fatigue. Adjust the number of repetitions you do to how you feel. Be disciplined enough to stay with your exercises when you're just feeling lazy, but do not push past exhaustion.

- Be aware that during pregnancy your body will take a little longer to warm up. You should also know that the uterus will press on organs and pull on ligaments as it grows larger unless you maintain correct posture throughout every movement. The oxygen you breathe, always a fuel for your body's work, now has to sustain two. So don't forget that warming up, doing the exercise correctly and proper breathing are important.

If you find that you exercise better with music and an instructor, you can order a double cassette or double album of the Pregnancy & Recovery Workout.

Send a check payable to The Workout for $12.00 for the Pregnancy & Recovery Workout double cassette and $13.00 for the Pregnancy & Recovery Workout double album. (Do write on your check which one you want.) Send to:

> The Workout
> P. O. Box 2957
> Beverly Hills, CA 90213

California residents add 6% sales tax. Canadian residents send U.S. funds and include an additional $3.00 for postage on all record orders.

POSTURE

For a woman with a well-balanced muscular system, good posture is an unconscious function, the result of a fine interplay between major muscle groups: the feet, the calves, the front of the thighs, the buttocks, the abdomen, the back, the top of the chest and shoulders and the neck. If you improve your posture in one area you will correct the other areas as well. Begin your warm-up by adjusting the position of your head.

One NECK AND SHOULDER STRETCHES

Starting position: Sit on a firm pillow with the legs folded in what we call "semi-lotus" position. Slip your right hand under your right buttock and lift it up and back so you are sitting squarely on the sitting bone. Do the same on the other side. Then stretch the crown of your head toward the ceiling.

1. With the spine in this extended position, let your head drop back, if possible so far that the back of your head touches your upper back. Allow your mouth to be pulled open.

Now stretch your lower jaw toward the ceiling, and pull your lower lip over the upper one. Relax your jaw then repeat slowly 8 to 10 times, thinking carefully about what you are doing, then return your head to a balanced position with the crown stretched to the ceiling.

Continued ⟶

NECK AND SHOULDER STRETCHES (continued)

2. With your spine thus extended, tuck your chin into the little pocket right above your clavicle. Interlace your fingers, place them on top of your skull, bring your elbows close together and allow the weight of your arms to give a steady stretch to the muscles along the back of your neck and down your spine. Hold this position for 20 seconds and concentrate on your breathing. Make it a relaxed even flow of air in and out. Then lift your head with the crown extended toward the ceiling again.

3. Let your head drop over your left shoulder stretching it toward the upper part of the wall to your left.

Place your right hand on your right shoulder to make sure that shoulder stays down. Place your left hand on the right side of your head over your ear and allow the weight of that hand to pull your head a little farther over toward your left shoulder. Pay attention to the even rhythm of your breathing and hold the stretch for twenty seconds. Then remove your hands, lift your head up, extend the crown to the ceiling and repeat this stretch with your head over your right shoulder.

4. With the crown of your head stretched toward the ceiling and the spine thus extended, inhale and, without involving the shoulders in the movement, turn your head to your right and exhale.

Inhale while returning to center, then turn your head to your left and exhale. Inhale to center.

Turn to the right again, exhale and this time slowly turn a little farther. Inhale to center, turn to the left, exhale and increase this turn. Inhale to center. Turn to the right, exhale, hold this position, inhale and with the next exhalation, slowly turn farther. Repeat on the left side. Then center and balance your head with the crown extended. Keep it there and allow the spine to realign itself.

Continued ⟶

NECK AND SHOULDER STRETCHES (continued)

5. Lift your shoulders up toward your ears and drop them down. Up, down, up, down, 8 times.

6. Pull your shoulders forward and push them back. Forward and back 8 times.

7. Then make big circles with the shoulders, a few circling forward and a few circling back.

During an exercise session and daily activities, try to move with the crown of your head lifted, keeping your shoulders relaxed. You will begin to move as gracefully as women who carry a water jug on their heads.

BREATHING

Still seated on the pillow, place both hands on your midriff and lift your rib cage as high as you can. Hold it high, relax your shoulders and balance your head. Your chin neither sticks out nor is tucked in. Rest your hands on your knees and allow your inner thighs to relax. Pay attention to your breathing. It will deepen a bit now that you have freed your diaphragm. Notice how your body expands as you breathe in and contracts as you breathe out. This movement is central to all physical and mental effort. Decide that you will not hold your breath as you work harder. If you do, you make it more difficult for your body to keep up with the increased demands. Your ability to continue to breathe evenly through strenuous work, whether exercise or labor, will increase when you improve your awareness of the muscles which assist the diaphragm in breathing.

One COMPLETE BREATHS

First practice a complete breath. With one hand on your abdomen and one on your chest, inhale and expand both abdomen and chest; then exhale. Toward the end of the exhalation, slowly lift your abdomen up and in. Inhale again by expanding slowly first the abdomen then the chest; then exhale by lifting the abdomen toward your back. Repeat a few more times. Equalize the duration of the breath in and out by counting: 1, 2, 3, 4 in; 1, 2, 3, 4 out. If possible inhale through your nose to filter, warm and moisten the air. Exhale whichever way is more comfortable. (You may feel a slight dizziness or vigorous stirring of the baby as a response to the unexpected increase in oxygen. Breathe a little slower and both symptoms will probably stop. If not, they will cease when you return to normal breathing.) A rate of four to six complete breaths per minute is good.

Two ABDOMINAL BREATHING

After four or five complete breaths, make a slight change in this breathing, this time keeping your lower abdominal muscles relaxed during an exhalation. When the abdomen is not pulled in and up, the exhalation is less complete and the inhalation which follows is less deep too. Do encourage your abdomen to move out with an inhalation but keep it uninvolved in the exhalations. Place both hands on the lower abdominal muscles to become aware of their response. During the uterine contractions of labor, it can be helpful to keep your lower abdominal muscles relaxed so the uterus can move more freely. Now aim for a rate of six to ten breaths per minute.

Three CHEST BREATHING

Next try to limit the use of skeletal muscles for breathing to those of the chest. Place both hands with the fingertips touching just below your breasts on your rib cage. Point your thumbs toward your back.

Inhale, separating your fingertips by expanding your ribs; exhale and allow your fingertips to touch again. Repeat a few times. Watch your abdomen. It will move slightly, but less than when it was actively involved in the breathing effort. Your breath is more superficial now and therefore faster. Between twelve and twenty breaths per minute is fine. Equalize the inhalation and exhalation again by counting. When an unconscious function like breathing becomes a conscious effort it may seem awkward at first, but try not to disturb the natural rhythm of your breathing.

Four PANTING

Now try breathing with even fewer skeletal muscles. Relax your jaws with the mouth slightly open. Rest your tongue with its tip against your lower front teeth, in the floor of your mouth where it will stay moist with the accumulation of saliva. Exhale audibly with a very slight push. Encourage the air which rushes back in to move over your moist tongue, thus preventing excessive dryness of the throat. Gently push the air out again and you will discover that after a slightly forced exhalation, inhaling quietly takes care of itself. Listen to the rhythm of audible breath and silence; it sounds like a child playing choo-choo trains. Your breath should be shallow and will therefore be rapid. The body moves slightly at the midriff which will make the abdomen and chest move a little too, but these regions are not intentionally involved in the breathing effort. Allow the very upper part of the chest to move gently too, but keep the shoulders relaxed. Speed up this panting to a rhythm of one exhalation per second and then slow it down again. Give the air as much time to rush in as to flow out.

Return to chest breathing, then to abdominal breathing and finish with a few complete breaths.

In applying these breathing techniques to exercise, you will exhale on the effort, during the contraction of whatever muscles are involved. Inhale when the muscles are in a more relaxed state. During strenuous work or exercise and at the peak of a labor contraction switch whenever necessary to a type of breathing which involves fewer skeletal muscles. Panting can be helpful during great physical effort or during the intense stretching caused by labor contractions.

WARM-UP AND DAILY EXERCISE ROUTINE

The increased levels of estrogen and progesterone which relax all muscles, including those not under conscious control (like the ones around the bowels and blood vessels) bear most of the responsibility for the sluggish circulation and fluid retention so common in pregnancy.

The warm-up prepares your body to work. Rhythmic movements wake up the muscles by improving their circulation. Smoothly rotating the joints, which may become slightly stiff with fluid, keeps them more flexible.

Therefore try to do the warm-up exercises routinely, every day if possible, and especially on days when you feel sluggish. Do them before you get dressed in the morning or right after an afternoon nap. These exercises are as essential a part of your care for yourself as bathing. Once warm-ups have become a routine, they will take less than ten minutes.

Adjust your posture first then practice the breathing exercises, paying attention to both your breath and your posture while you warm up.

One WRISTS AND HANDS

Starting position: Sit in semi-lotus position, arms lifted to the front, parallel with the shoulders, elbows locked.

1. Bend your wrists, lifting your fingers up to the ceiling,

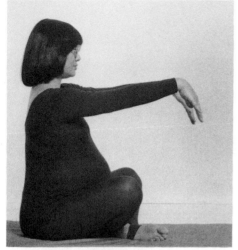

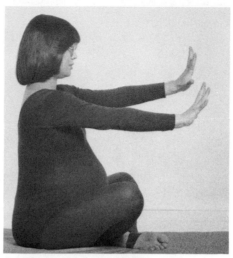

. . . then pointing them down to the floor. Repeat a few times.

2. Draw large circles with your hands, a few to the right, then to the left.

3. Allow your arms to bend slightly at your elbows, make fists, and throw your fingers out. Repeat a few times.

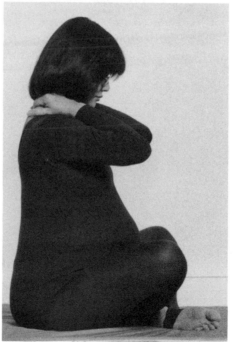

4. Vigorously rub your hands together. Place your now-relaxed fingers on the bridge of your nose. Stroke up and over your forehead, make small circular movements at your temples, then a bit lower where your jaws meet. Grasp your ears as your fingers slide over them with a little pull up and back.

5. Then slide your fingers down your neck to knead the top of your shoulders firmly and pleasantly.

Two ARM STRETCHES

Starting position: Sit in semi-lotus, left arm stretched up to the ceiling.

1. Bend your left arm at the elbow, dropping your hand down your back.

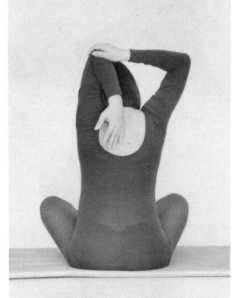

2. Place your right hand on your left upper arm close to the elbow. Lift your left elbow with your right hand and gently pull it so your left hand can slide a bit farther down the middle of your back.

3. Swing your right arm around and grasp your left hand behind your back. Hold this stretch with unstrained breath for 20 seconds. Reverse arm positions and repeat.

Three THE CHEST EXPANDER

Starting position: Sit in semi-lotus, the back of your hands placed against your middle back, the knuckles in line with the bottom edge of your shoulder blades.

Slowly turn your palms together, allowing the elbows to move out and back. The crown of your head continues to reach for the ceiling. Notice how this position opens the chest and frees the diaphragm. Hold this stretch with relaxed breathing for 20 seconds, then relax.

Four THE TWIST

Starting position: Sit in semi-lotus, with the buttocks pulled back, the upper body lifted off the midriff and the crown of the head extended.

Exhale and turn your upper body to the right. Place your right hand behind you on the floor and your left hand on your right knee. Use the left hand as a lever to turn your upper body farther, thus stretching the muscles at the waist. Inhale and return to a centered position. Exhale and turn to the left. Repeat 4–5 times to each side.

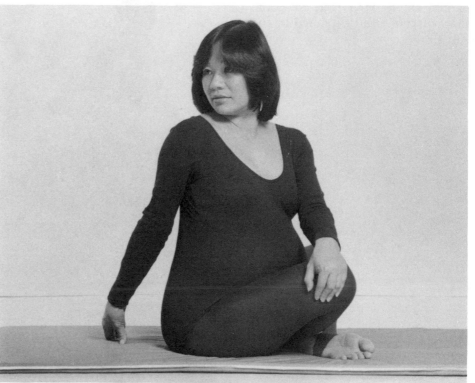

Five LEG STRETCHES

Starting position: Sit on the sitting bones, legs straight out in front, midriff lifted, crown of head extended.

1. Gently bend and straighten alternately the right and left knees. When straightening, stretch your heel away and pull your toes toward your body.

2. After a few repetitions, straighten both legs and lock your knees. Exhale, pull your toes toward your body, push your heels away and lift them slightly. Inhale, point your toes away.

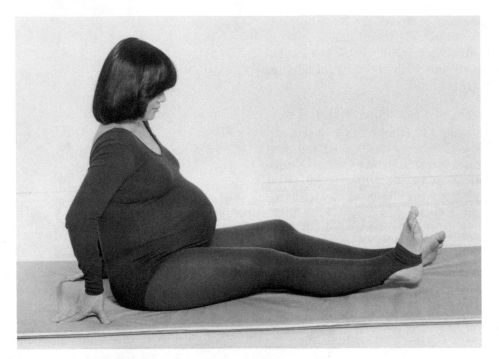

3. Make fists and place them so the phalanges between your knuckles and the first finger joints are against your lower back. Rub this area with good pressure while continuing to flex and extend your feet. Keep the crown of your head extended to the ceiling.

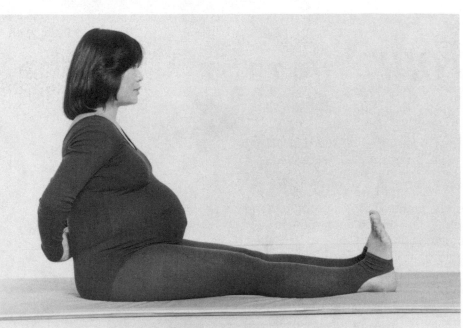

Six ANKLES AND FEET

Starting position: Sit in semi-lotus with the crown of the head extended. Take one leg in both hands, and pull it close to the body.

1. Rotate your foot at the ankle a few times to the left then to the right. Make these rotations as large as possible, stretching to your maximum.

2. Without moving the foot at the ankle, pull your toes open and toward your body, then bend them away and curl them tight. Repeat a few times, then do these movements with your other leg.

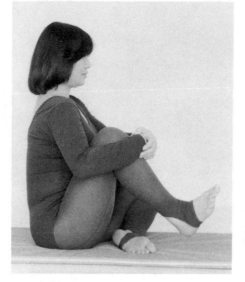 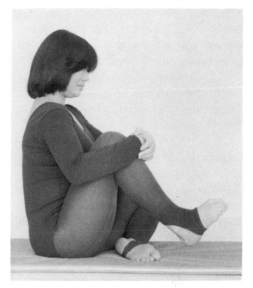

Seven THIGH STRETCHER

Starting position: Sit with knees bent, the soles of your feet touching and the heels as close to your body as possible. Make sure your buttocks have not slipped under and that the crown of your head is still extended. Place your hands on your ankles.

Lean straight forward, spine erect. Keeping your midriff lifted and without rounding your shoulders, gently press your knees closer to the floor with your elbows. Hold this stretch—but not your breath—for 20 seconds; relax and repeat.

Eight THE ANGRY CAT

Starting position: Kneel with the body weight equally distributed between the hands and knees. Make sure your arms and legs are like posts, forming right angles at the shoulder and hip joints and at the floor, supporting your body at these four corners.

Exhale, drop head and buttocks under and pull your back up. (Cats do this very gracefully.) Inhale, look up and relax your back, as in the starting position, without allowing it to sag. Repeat 8 to 10 times.

Nine CAT TWISTS

Starting position: Kneel with the weight equally distributed between the hands and the knees.

Exhale and turn your right shoulder toward your right hip. You should feel a stretch at the left side of your waist. Inhale and return to the center. Exhale and turn your left shoulder toward your left hip. Inhale and return to center. Repeat, alternating sides, 8 to 10 times each.

Ten CAT STRETCHES

Starting position: Kneel with the weight equally distributed between the hands and the knees.

Exhale, lift your left arm and your right leg and stretch them away from each other. Reach with your fingers and your heel. Keep your arm and leg parallel to the floor in a straight line with your body, and look at the floor. Inhale, put them down.

Exhale, then lift and stretch your right arm and left leg in the same way. When your balance becomes steadier, pick up speed and lift and stretch, alternating sides, 8 to 10 times each.

Eleven PELVIC TONER

Starting position: Kneel with elbows on the floor, chin on your hands, and buttocks up—this is the "knee-chest position" in which the uterus falls away from the pelvic floor.

Contract the muscles along the rectum, the vagina and the labia. Hold a few counts, relax, then contract again with the image of closing the vagina while lifting it inward. Repeat 10 to 15 times.

THE PREGNANCY WORKOUT

When your body is in optimal condition you will have endurance, strength and flexibility. Endurance is built by repetitious movements. Muscles only improve their function when they are asked to, so you will increase your number of repetitions each day. But muscle recovery time is short. Resting more than a minute within a series is like starting anew. Therefore, rest breaks within each particular exercise should be brief. Stop to shake out a muscle when necessary but return to the movement immediately if you feel you can do more. Watch yourself in the mirror. When your muscles tire, do the exercise with *more* rather than less precision. When this becomes impossible, rest a few moments and move on to the next exercise.

You can judge how many repetitions to do by your ability to maintain the correct technique during your workout as well as by the duration of muscle soreness after a session. If you feel no discomfort, your muscles have been maintained in good condition. Sore stiffness lasting up to twenty-four hours means the muscle was pushed to improve. Soreness that lasts longer indicates the muscle was worked a little too hard.

To ease soreness, take a warm bath and knead gently the worked muscles—the improved circulation carries away the waste products. It will help too to drink a lot of water—a glass on the hour, every hour. Do not exercise a muscle again until the soreness is gone.

While a steadily increasing number of rhythmic repetitions improves endurance, strength is built by working against a gradually increased amount of resistance. During pregnancy you won't need weights because the baby steadily increases your body weight.

Once lost, flexibility is only slowly and painfully regained. Stretching is an art—don't confuse it with straining or pulling. Allow your body to go only as far into a stretch as it can while maintaining correct posture. Greater flexibility will come with better muscle tone. Stretch gently and steadily. Dancers, who do a tremendous amount of stretching, may seem at first glance to bounce to stretch, but on a closer look you will notice the dancer places her body then stretches, places it again and stretches. Each time the dancer places her body in a position to incorporate the gain from the stretch. These subtle movements require less strength than holding a position steadily for a length of time. Exhale as you stretch and inhale as you place your body correctly. Learn to hold a stretch for increasingly long periods. Aim first for ten seconds and slowly work up to twenty. Attend to your breathing and make it an easy, effortless flow. When your breathing is tense, your body tenses.

The pregnancy workout is divided into four sections: Upper Body, Waist, Legs and Feet, and Pelvic Region. Within each section you will work on endurance and strength first then move on to stretching. The full workout will take close to an hour. On days when you don't have quite that much time, do the warm-up, then the four exercises marked with an asterisk(*). Those four work the major muscle groups quite well.

THE UPPER BODY

Your upper body will need a lot of attention during pregnancy for these reasons: First, exercising the arms improves the circulation and therefore the function of the breasts; second, a strong upper body resists better the temptation to lean on the lower half; third, the increased weight of the breasts, combined with the pull of the pregnant uterus on your posture, can cause upper back aches almost as frequently as pain in the lower back; fourth, a new mother needs strong arms to carry her baby and lots of equipment; and finally, when nursing, changing, and otherwise tending to the baby, you will spend a lot of time bent forward with your upper body. As a result, many new mothers suffer tension in the neck, upper back and shoulders. When these muscles are strong and flexible, caring for your infant will cause much less strain.

One CHEST EXPANDER

Starting position: Stand tall, feet about hip distance apart and parallel, arms bent at right angles, lifted to the side, elbows parallel with shoulders.

Exhale and bring the arms together in front of your chest. Inhale and open them wide. Keep your elbows level with your shoulders. Work up to 24 repetitions.

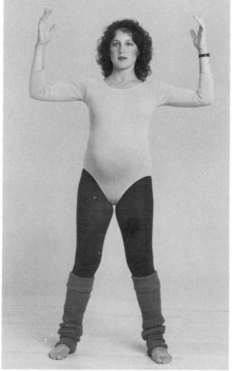

Two UPPER ARM TONER

Starting position: Stand tall, feet about hip distance apart and parallel, arms extended to the sides and held at shoulder level with palms up and open.

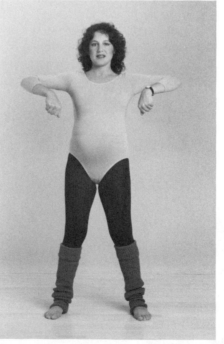

1. Exhale, make fists, bend elbows and bring your fists in toward the shoulders.

2. Your palms within the fists will face the floor. Keeping your elbows at shoulder level, now drop the fists to either side of your rib cage,

3. then straighten the arms again by pushing fists back out to shoulder level. The palms will now face backwards.

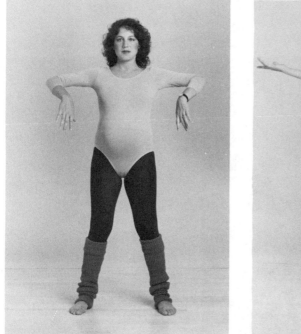

4. Reverse by bringing your forearms and fists back in to the rib cage and shoulders, then open your palms

5. and stretch your arms back to the starting position. The upper arms should hardly move as your forearms draw these circles. Work up to 24 repetitions.

Three ARM FLINGS

Starting position: Stand tall, feet about hip distance apart and parallel, arms crossed in front of the chest, elbows at shoulder height.

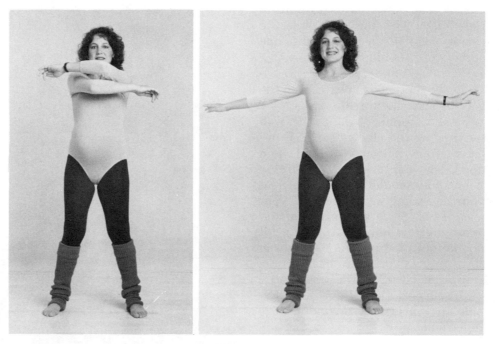

1. Inhale and open your arms with your elbows still bent, then swing your elbows open and your arms all the way back.

2. Exhale and cross them in front of the chest again, and repeat from there. Work up to 24 repetitions.

Four WALL PUSH-UPS*

Starting position: Face a wall, standing slightly more than arm's length away from it with the feet parallel, about hip distance apart. Lean forward and place your palms on the wall slightly below shoulder level, fingers pointing in toward opposite hand.

1. Bring your nose to the wall by letting your body come forward in a straight line. Your arms bend at the elbows, the lower arms forming a right angle with the wall while the upper arms form a straight line across your shoulders.

2. Push your body away from the wall by straightening the arms.

Repeat, coming toward the wall by bending the elbows again. Don't leave your buttocks behind, and don't let your heels come off the floor. You should feel a stretch at your chest and at the back of your legs. If not, place your arms farther apart and/or move your feet a bit farther away from the wall. If in spite of best efforts your heels lift up, step a bit closer to the wall. Settle into a slow rhythm of push-ups. Exhale up. Inhale down. Work up to 24 repetitions.

Five THE TOUGH STRETCH

You will find this stretch a little more difficult, but work on it because it is important.

Starting position: Stand tall with your feet together and parallel. Place the back of your open hands with your little fingers together against the upper back at your shoulder blades.

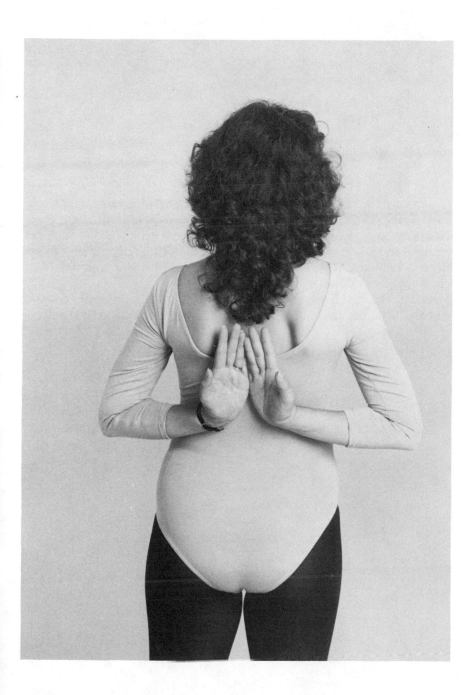

1. Turn your palms and fingers together by bending your elbows back. Maintain the image of extending the crown of your head.

Continued ⟶

THE TOUGH STRETCH (continued)

2. Turn your left foot 45° to the left. Step forward with your right foot.

3. Now reach with the crown of your head forward and bend from your hips with a flat back. Think about your breathing and allow your chest, your arms and the back of your legs to stretch. Keep your elbows up and out to open the chest and ease the pressure at the little fingers.

4. At the point of maximum stretch, drop your head. Hold this position, concentrating deeply on your stretch, then come up and do the exercise again with the feet reversed.

If the pain at the little fingers and the wrists is too great, fold the arms behind the back instead of turning the palms together. The stretch in the chest and the opening up of the region of the diaphragm won't be as great, but in time you'll be able to keep your palms together. Slowly increase the time you hold the stretch to 20 seconds.

THE WAIST

Your waist may have disappeared temporarily but your waist muscles are still there. They can be worked by a rhythmic turning of the upper body. These alternating trunk rotations improve poor circulation to the liver and irregularity with bowel movements, two frequent problems during gestation. If you have a tendency toward constipation do extra waist turns daily—these and The Twist (see page 47) from the warm-up.

One SIDE TURNS

Starting position: Give your body a balanced foundation by placing your feet parallel and a bit more than hip distance apart. Bend your knees slightly and shift most of your body weight onto your left leg. Turn your right foot out 45° and allow this foot to stabilize your balance, but keep most of your weight on the left leg. Extend the crown of your head to the ceiling and lift your body up from your hips. Lift your bent arms until your elbows are slightly below shoulder level.

1. Turn from the waist first a bit to the left . . .

2. and then as far as possible to the right. Use your arms to move and guide the turns. Do keep your hips parallel to each other; do not allow the one which carries most of the weight to sag. Inhale for the small turn to the left, exhale for the larger turn to the right, and stretch a bit farther with each repetition. After the seventh month, or when the

uterus gets large, do not try to stretch with each turn. Instead, turn gently and rhythmically.

After 16 to 24 turns, shake your legs out and repeat the exercise with your right leg as the weight carrier and your left one as the stabilizer. Now inhale on the small turn to the right, then exhale as you turn to the left, stretching a bit more with each exhalation.

Two SIDE STRETCHES

Starting position: Place your feet parallel and more than hip distance apart. Extend your arms to the sides and raise them parallel with your shoulders. Keeping your hips facing front, turn your left foot 90° to the left and your right foot 30° to the left. Lift your body up from your hips while making sure the hips are still facing the original forward direction.

1. Push your hips to the right and lean with your upper body to the left.

2. Slowly lean farther over the left side. Allow your left hand to slide down your left leg, past your knee if possible. Raise your right hand toward the ceiling and slowly stretch your hands away from each other, keeping them parallel with the chest. Both hips continue to face forward.

3. Hold the stretch with relaxed breathing, or switch to a light panting if necessary and look up at the hand which reaches for the ceiling. Realign your hips and shoulders if you feel a strain in the lower back.

Repeat this stretch to the right with the same precision. Slowly improve your ability to hold the end position on each side for 20 seconds.

THE LEGS AND THE FEET

Before working the pelvis, the region which carries the bulk of the changes of pregnancy, birth and recovery, strengthen and stretch your feet and calves. They carry all the extra weight. And tightness and lack of circulation in the calf muscles will make you more prone to the painful leg cramps which are quite common during pregnancy. If such cramps have wakened you at night do this exercise before you go to bed. Leg cramps can also be caused by an imbalance in the trace minerals in your system, so discuss your diet with a good nutritionist.

One LEG AND FOOT TONERS*

Starting position: Stand with your feet parallel and together on a large block or a thick book with the heels stretched over the edge. Face the wall and place your hands on a doorknob or against the wall for balance.

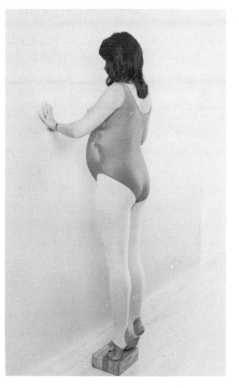 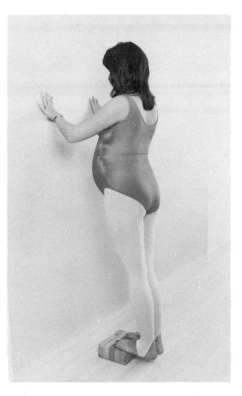

1. Come up on your toes ...

2. then lower your heels until they go below the edge of the block. Come way up on the toes again, then lower the heels down a little farther.

The hips are parallel and the major work is done by the legs. Exhale and go up; inhale and go down. Work up to 24 repetitions. Finish with the heels over the edge, slowly stretching them closer to the floor. Hold this stretch for 20 seconds.

THE PELVIC REGION

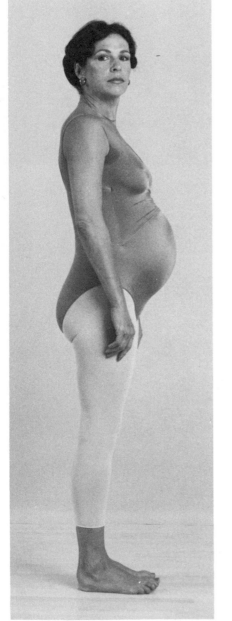

The upright posture which we humans enjoy has expanded our field of vision and freed our hands, and seems an evolutionary development to be grateful for, except perhaps during pregnancy and even more during childbirth, when the consequences of this change in posture—the mother's firmly closed cervix and her strong sling of muscles from pubic bone to lower back (both necessary for carrying a baby when we walk upright) and the increased diameter of the infant's head—cause the great labor of birth.

The drastic change in our posture for walking was followed, with the invention of chairs, by a change in our posture of sitting. Squatting has disappeared in our culture as an acceptable position for rest or for work, and with it went the stretching and strengthening of the muscles which kept the pelvis mobile.

Then woman, desiring a birdlike walk and wishing to heighten her allure and thrust her pelvis into an inviting position, altered her muscle structure still further by wearing high heels.

Orthodontia for the pelvis has not yet been invented, but exercises to counterbalance the negative effects of our habits have.

To check your posture in the pelvic area, stand tall with your feet parallel and together and look sideways in the mirror. Notice how the buttocks form rounded hills which rise out of the gentle curve of the lower back. This curve and the one in the upper back are part of the spine's structure; as living arches they give the spine a strength of its own. But these spinal modulations should only be slight, even in pregnancy when the pull of the heavy uterus tends to increase the one in the lower back. The correction of a painful dip to a gentle curve is not as simple as tucking the buttocks under. It is a process of realignment, of a balanced strengthening and stretching of all major posture muscles to allow the body to rediscover its proper balance. Thus in spite of the temptation to work primarily on the pelvic region to make the birth easier and to counteract the major weight gain on the hips, buttocks and thighs, do not work just this section and neglect the other parts.

One PELVIC ALIGNERS

Starting position: Place your feet a little more than hip distance apart, parallel, and bend your knees slightly. Extend your arms to the sides, lift your body up from your hips and off your midriff and extend the crown of your head to the ceiling.

1. Tuck the pelvis under, then release it, not from the lower back but by using the same muscles you used to tuck under.

2. After 12 to 15 repetitions, turn your feet out and continue to tuck under and release your pelvis. You should feel a slight stretch now at the inner thighs when you tuck your pelvis under. (Look down to make sure the big and second toes are visible on the inside of each bent knee.) Slowly bend the knees farther, then return to slightly bent knees while tucking and releasing the pelvis. Work up to 24 repetitions.

Continued ⟶

PELVIC ALIGNERS (continued)

3. Move your hips sideways instead of forward and back. Lift your right hip and drop it down . . .

. . . then the left one and drop it down. Keep your feet turned out only if correct turnout (the two inner toes visible inside both knees) can be maintained.

Otherwise place them parallel with the knees still bent slightly to protect the lower back. Repeat 12 to 15 times.

4. Circle the hips to the side and forward, to the other side and back.

Repeat 8 times, reverse directions and circle 8 times again.

Two TRUNK STRETCHES

Starting position: Stand with feet hip distance apart and at a comfortable turnout, arms raised gracefully.

Lift your rib cage up from your hips and your waist and move it to the right . . .

. . . then lift it up over the uterus and to the left.

Move right, left, right, left. The shoulders will move but the main effort comes from the muscles at the waist and the abdomen. Repeat 16 times.

Three PLIÉS

Starting position: Stand with your feet a little more than hip distance apart and turned out (correct your turnout if necessary by making sure that you can see the inner two toes on each foot inside your bent knees). Extend the crown of your head up to the ceiling and raise your arms to the sides or drop them gracefully in front of you.

1. Bend your knees out over your feet, then straighten them. Repeat 8 times.

2. Rise up on your toes . . .

. . . bend your knees,

. . . lower your heels, pressing them forward as you lower them,

. . . then straighten your legs, working for balance. Repeat 12 times.

3. Stay up on your toes with your knees bent over your turned-out feet so your big toe and the next one are visible on the inside of each knee, and bounce gently up and down. Let your arms relax gracefully in front of your body. Come a little farther down with each bounce to stretch the inner thighs and to loosen the hips. Continue to check for correct turnout and do not let your buttocks stick out. Relax and shake the legs out.

Four LEG SWINGS

Starting position: Stand on a block or book, place your left hand on the wall for support and let your right leg hang over the edge of the block. Make small rotations with the right leg from the hip and notice how this relaxes hip muscles and the hip joint. Do not let your pelvis tilt, keep your hips parallel to the floor and lift your body up from the supporting hip. Keep the knee of the supporting leg soft (not extended) and do not sag toward this hip.

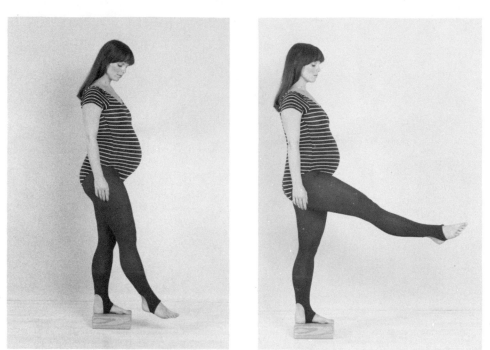

1. Turn your right foot out, straighten and extend the knee, and lift this leg to the front, then bring it down. Watch your posture. Repeat 12 times.

2. Move the right leg out to the side and bring it in next to the left. Repeat 12 times.

3. Move the right leg to the back and outward at a diagonal of 45° and bring it in again. Move only the leg, not the pelvis. Repeat 12 times.

Take a little time to let the hip of the standing leg relax by swinging it and rotating it over the edge of the block, then turn around to work the other leg.

Five DIVE SQUATS*

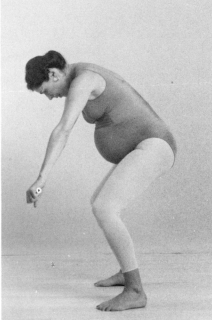

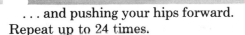

Starting position: With the feet parallel and about hip distance apart, come down into a squat with the thighs parallel to the floor. Stretch your arms and your upper body forward as if preparing to dive.

Make fists and pull your fists to your hips, letting your torso come up . . .

. . . and pushing your hips forward. Repeat up to 24 times.

Then squat down with your feet parallel or turned out, your knees over your toes. (Try to place your feet flat on the floor.) Rest your arms on your knees, relax into this squat and rest for a few moments.

Six KNEELING LEG LIFTS*

Starting position: Kneel on all fours, with your hands shoulder distance apart well under your chest on the floor.

1. Raise your left knee to the side, your knee higher than your foot, and drop it down. Distribute your weight equally between your right leg and your left arm.

2. Then lift this leg to the back and drop it down, keeping your knee bent. Keep your body still and move only your leg. Let it swing freely from your hip.

Work up to 24 repetitions, lifting to the side and to the back alternately. When you feel strong enough follow that with 24 lifts to the side, then 24 lifts to the back. Rest with your chin on your hands and your buttocks up in the air. Then work your right leg in the same way. Rest again with your chin on your hands and your buttocks up.

Seven   *BODY SWINGS*

Starting position: Kneel, with your body erect. Place your open hands on your lower abdomen, touching the front of your hipbones. Lift your knee caps gently to free them in the same way you lift the buttocks to free the sitting bones.

Let your body swing gently back and forth from your knees as if it is blowing in the wind. Keep a straight line from the knees to the forehead. The abdominal and thigh muscles do most of the work, but the buttocks work too. Watch your profile for that straight line, especially between the front of your thighs and the front of your hip bones. Work up to 15 repetitions.

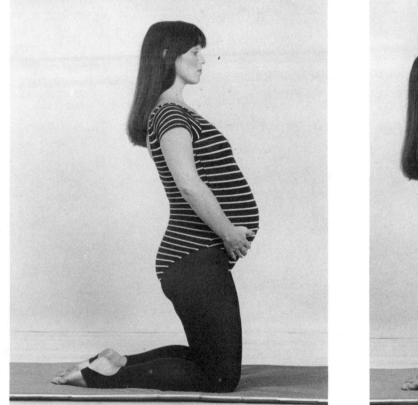 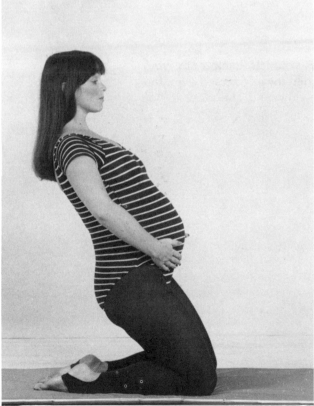

Eight THE LAID-BACK STRETCH

Starting position: On your knees, your body erect, sit down between your calves with your heels against your outer thighs and your big toes close to your body. Place one or two pillows so they will fill the curve in the small of the back when you lie down.

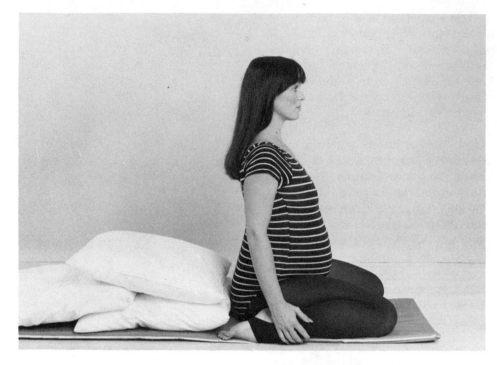

1. Lower yourself back onto your elbows, then lower yourself even farther. Lie down all the way, if you can.

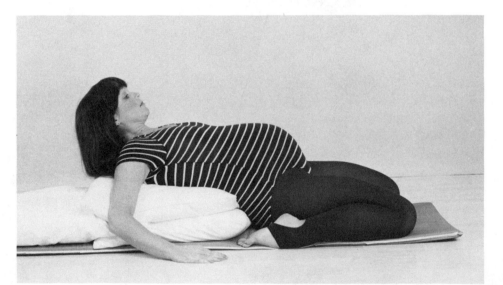

2. Relax into this stretch, breathing easily for 20 to 30 seconds, and come up slowly, first onto your elbows then all the way.

Variation:

Those of you who are not flexible enough for this exercise should stretch one leg at a time. Sit with one leg straight and the other bent next to you then lower yourself slowly and relax into the stretch. Come up to reverse the position of the legs for a stretch on the other side.

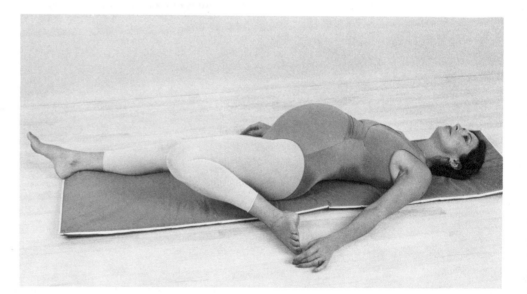

Nine SMALL PELVIC TUCKS

Starting position: Sit with your legs straight and stretched wide apart. Lift each buttock up and back, then place your hands behind your buttocks on the floor and straighten your body.

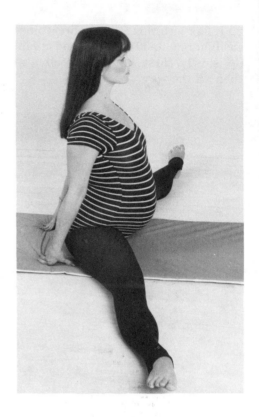

1. Very gently rock your pelvis using the same muscles as in the standing Pelvic Aligners. It is a more difficult and smaller movement when seated, but it helps to loosen the pelvis at the hips and strengthen the lower back. Tuck and release without expecting to see much of a difference between the positions.

2. After 20 or so repetitions, place your hands in between your legs. Now flex and point your feet; flex and point. Stretch your heels away with each flexing of your feet . . .

. . . and open your legs a little wider with each pointing of your toes.

Continued ⟶

SMALL PELVIC TUCKS (continued)

3. After 10 to 15 repetitions, pull up and back on your buttocks once more and open your legs, toes pointed, as far as you can. Then lift your body up from your hips and "walk" your hands forward between your legs. Keep your spine straight while you bring your chest as close to the floor as you can.

Rest and relax at the point of maximum stretch then let your hands walk your body back up. Bring your legs together and shake them out.

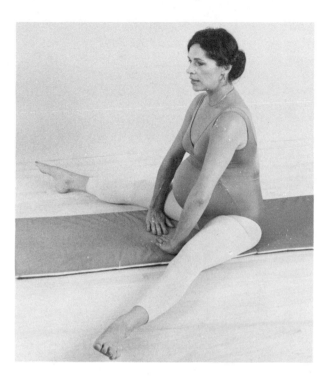

When doing these Small Pelvic Tucks, be careful!

Do not stretch your legs wider than is comfortable . . .

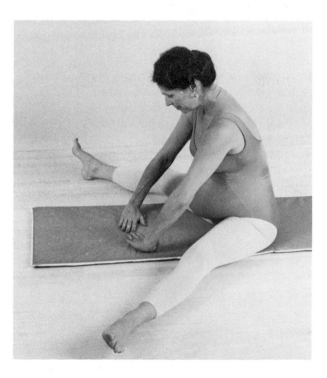

. . . and do not force your body farther forward than your flexibility allows.

Ten *THIGH TONER*

Starting position: Sit with the soles of your feet together and as close to your body as possible. Lift your buttocks up and back and straighten your body up from your hips. Place your hands on your ankles.

1. Lean forward and allow your bending elbows to press gently on your inner thighs near your knees, or on your lower legs from the knees down. Let your legs stretch open at the pelvis and concentrate on your breathing. Hold this stretch for 20 seconds.

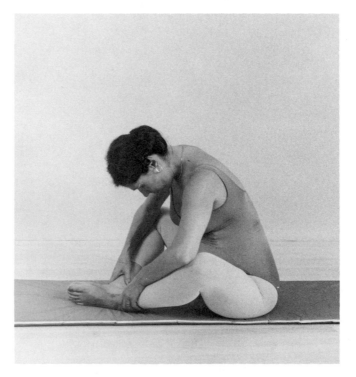

2. With your knees still bent and your soles close to your body, place your hands on your inner thighs. Bring your thighs together slowly but resist this movement with your hands.

3. Then place your hands on your outer thighs. Open your legs slowly, now resisting their opening with your hands.

Repeat this inward and outward movement of the legs against resistance 8 times. Shake your legs out and get ready for a few minutes of deep relaxation.

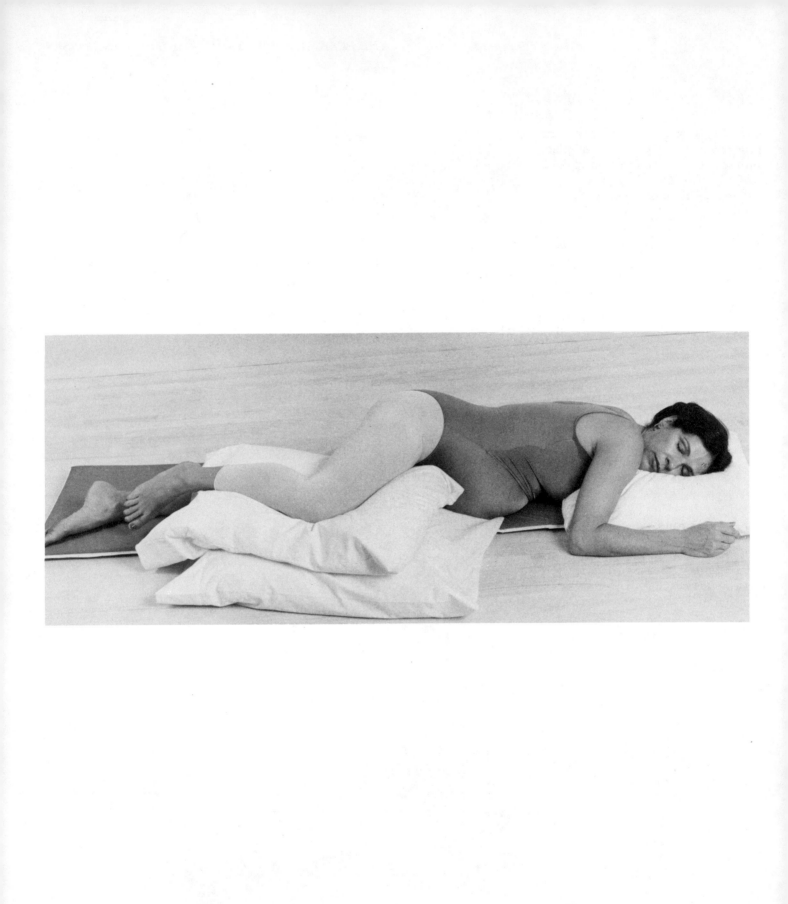

RELAXATION TECHNIQUES

In yoga, the "corpse pose" is as essential a part of strengthening the body for the challenges of life as are any of the active poses. This deep relaxation allows the body to harvest the energy released during the stretches for its own internal purposes. The mind, alerted to the body's functioning by concentrating on doing the postures correctly, is more in unity with the body than it is at most other times, and a very deep relaxation with further integration of body and mind results.

During pregnancy an exercise session should always be followed by a few minutes of deep relaxation. Of course the body needs the energy and the mind the increased body awareness in order to cope better with the fast changes, but, more important, deep relaxation is the core of all the techniques for handling labor and should be practiced routinely during pregnancy.

Lie down on your exercise pad or on a very firm mattress so your spine will be well supported when you relax. Turn on your left side to keep the uterus off the vena cava, the major vessel returning blood to your heart. In this position your body can function with the least amount of effort. Straighten your bottom leg and fold the top one over on a pillow. Place your left arm behind your body down along your back. Support your breasts and your uterus with soft flat pillows if necessary and place a thicker pillow under your head. Move about and make adjustments until you feel comfortable. Then close your eyes and concentrate on your breathing.

As you inhale allow your chest to expand. As you exhale, allow any tension to flow out of your chest with the air. With the next inhalation, let your abdomen and your chest open up and with this exhalation let the tension flow out of the abdomen as well. When the air moves in again, picture your arms and your legs as opening with this expansion. When the air moves out, let arm and leg tension flow out with the air. With the next inhalation let this image of opening with the incoming air spread to your fingertips and your toes; with the air moving out, breathe all tension out of the farthest corners of your body. Inhale deeply once more, now allowing your shoulders, your neck and your head to open to the fresh flow of air. Then as you exhale, breathe any tension out of these parts. Inhale slowly and consciously with the intent of letting the oxygen reach your brain. Then as you exhale, breathe away your stale thoughts as well. Repeat this a few times, then slowly turn your mind inward to scan your body. Do you notice tension anywhere which you might be able to release? Notice how your body rests heavier on the mat or mattress.

Focus on the muscles which move your jaws, and relax them deeply. Your mouth falls open a bit and your lips relax. Relax your jaw muscles even more. Then allow this relaxation to spread over your face, down your neck and into your shoulders. Now focus on your shoulders for a few moments. Relax all the muscles which move your arms. They are in the front of your chest, at the top of your shoulders and in your upper back. Let this relaxation spread down your arms to your hands and your fingers. Then allow your concentration to drift to your chest, down and around your waist to your hips. Stop here to focus on relaxing the muscles which move your legs. They are in your lower abdomen, in your lower back and buttocks, in your groin and around your thighs. Let this relaxation spread down your legs past your knees and calves to your feet and toes. Let your mind return up along your legs to the triangular bone at your very lower back. Picture your spine—the loosely stacked vertebrae with nerves coming in and going out through the openings in between them and muscle columns supporting each side. Relax those muscles. Start at your lower back, then move up to the area of your waist and after a short pause there, focus on the region in between your shoulders, then move up to where your neck enters your head. Now allow your mind to reflect on itself. It is never still. Thoughts well up, sounds and sensations are registered. Notice those disturbances and fluctuations. Acknowledge a sensation and decide whether it needs attention. If not, continue to stay deeply relaxed and aware of the interaction of body and mind, then of the depth of the mind. The sensations it registers are mere surface ripplings of a pond whose depth and breadth we cannot measure.

After a few minutes deepen your breath and notice how this reactivates your body. Move your feet, your hands, your legs, your arms. Roll your head from side to side and come up to a sitting position.

Full lotus position

Semi-lotus position

Sit on a firm pillow again and lift your buttocks up and back. Fold your legs in complete lotus or semi-lotus position and rest your hands on your knees. Lift your body up from your midriff and extend the crown of your head toward the ceiling. Cast your eyes down along the tip of your nose. Count your breaths and see if you can reach a count of eight. Each time you catch your mind wandering, start at the count of one again. You will begin to notice a stillness within, a solitude. The mystery of our life and its strength lies within each of us. Finding this source of inspiration is always important, but for a woman who is becoming a mother, it is essential. It helps her resume the activities of the day with a feeling of strength. Try to finish each exercise session with a few minutes of such meditation.

PREPARATION
FOR NURSING

A woman's breasts usually fill with milk without any conscious effort. They do so in response to the hormone changes following birth and to the stimulus of the baby's suckling. The quality of this milk has yet to be matched by laboratory products, and the softness and warmth of a woman's breast cannot be duplicated by a plastic bottle and nipple. A mother and her nursing baby experience a great deal of pleasure. Therefore don't reject nursing too readily and don't see it as a difficult task. Instead, keep an open mind and if you aren't sure, wait to decide whether or not you will nurse until you first hold your infant and watch it search for your breasts.

You should begin to prepare for nursing fairly early in your pregnancy. What is your skin's general response to friction? Does it toughen easily, or is it inclined to feel sore when rubbed? If the latter, then you can toughen the skin on the nipple and the areola by friction and exposure to sun and wind. There are lots of ways to increase friction on the nipples. If you cut small holes in the cups of a bra you will have both breast support and friction as clothes rub against the nipples. Or massage the nipples in a circular motion with a wet washcloth working up to fifty strokes, and continue this circular rubbing with a towel while drying yourself and again work up to fifty strokes. Then there is friction during lovemaking. Always treat the breasts gently; glandular tissue should not be bruised or be compressed consistently in one area. Your choice of bra is very important—it should support but not press, bind, or constrict.

Do exercise your breasts by working your arms and by doing push-ups against the wall. This will strengthen the muscles of the chest wall and improve the function of your breasts.

Also check the ability of your nipples to become erect. Do they protrude when the breasts are cold or caressed or do they remain hidden? If they do not become readily visible, stretch the nipple tissue regularly, starting early in the pregnancy, if possible. Place the thumb and the index finger of one hand on the opposite sides of the outer margin of the areola, then slide thumb and index finger farther apart. Reach into the groove thus created with three fingers and the thumb of the other hand, take the nipple and gently pull, then twist one way and the other. Allow the nipple to stretch. Treat both breasts, then put on a well-fitting bra from which you have cut away the tips around the nipples. Gently try to pull the nipples through the openings.

Toward the end of your pregnancy learn how to express fluid from the breasts. Place the fingertips under and the thumb above the areola. Now roll the thumbs over the fingertips and over the breast tissue between them, first toward the chest then forward to the nipple. During nursing the baby exerts a similar suction as it holds the nipple between its palate and tongue. Such manual expression during pregnancy may sometimes yield the yellowish fluid called colostrum. If it does, just wipe it away, your body will continue to produce it. If it does not, don't worry. Women's breasts don't all start production at the same time.

And finally, be aware of the overall texture of your breasts. If you tend to develop lumps in certain areas, learn where they are and on days when the breasts are not too tender, massage them well. First place the open hands at the base of the breast and let them slide toward the nipple. Continue these strokes from the base of the breast to the nipple with smooth pressure for six to eight rhythmic repetitions. Then depending on its size, take this breast in one or in both hands, lift it and rotate the hand(s) and consequently the breast.

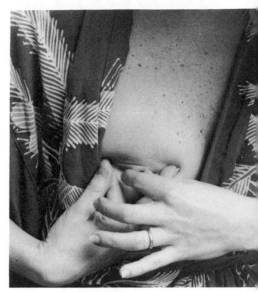

Take the nipple and gently pull . . .

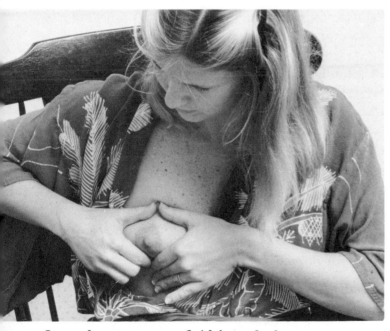

Learn how to express fluid from the breasts . . .

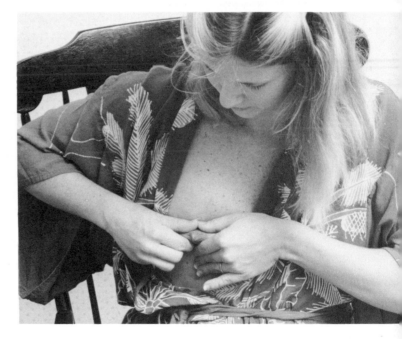

SPECIAL PROBLEMS

During pregnancy many women become increasingly sensitive. They experience rapid ups and downs, seemingly without external cause. Some say it's the hormones, others the change in appearance, which result in increasing vulnerability and dependency, although I think it can be both, and one more—concern for the child within. A pregnant woman seems more and more aware of the outer world, wondering if it will be good enough for her child. You may feel alternately depressed or elated, depending on what you see. Treat your own sensitivity with respect, but try to steer a clear course through the peaks and valleys of your feelings. While others will be supportive, still you will have to rely heavily on your own strength and courage to carry you through the difficult times.

Next to concern for the baby, most women worry about their rapidly changing bodies. Will my breasts sag, they ask, will I get stretch marks and will my belly ever be flat again?

The answers to the first two questions are complex because those changes appear to be partly genetic and partly nutritional. And the nutritional aspect is not determined as much by what you ate today as by what your mother ate when she carried you, and what you have eaten since. By improving your nutrition today, you cannot quite undo poor eating during adolescence but you are taking a step toward improvement and you are giving your child a better foundation.

Some women believe that wearing a support bra during the period of breast enlargement from pregnancy and lactation will prevent overstretching of the skin and sagging breasts. There is no evidence that this is correct. Therefore women who are more comfortable without a bra should probably not bother.

Keep in mind when buying your pregnancy bras that breast size usually reaches its peak in the seventh or the eighth month. A bra which fits then will also fit for nursing if you allow for the fact that the circumference of the chest will be smaller after the baby has arrived. To make a comfortable pregnancy bra handy for nursing, cut the shoulder straps from the cups and use velcro or a safety pin to fasten them again.

I'm not sure that it's true that the skin stretches more easily if it is rubbed regularly with oil or a vitamin E ointment, but the treatment can't hurt. Heat the oil and massage the skin of the breasts, the abdomen, the hips and the thighs in a kneading fashion a couple of times a week. If it does not keep stretch marks away, it will at least make the skin smooth and less inclined to become itchy. Should red marks appear on your skin, don't forget that they will become less visible after the baby is born, when they will shrink and become silvery white.

The question about a flat belly is easily answered: exercise. I have seen many women with flatter stomachs one year after childbirth than before they conceived, because during pregnancy they got into the habit of exercising regularly.

The common darkening of the skin around the nipples and elsewhere on the body will fade, and the dark line on the belly will disappear with time after the baby is born. If you notice a tendency for such skin discoloration during your pregnancy, you may want to avoid exposing your face to a sunbath at midday since bright sunlight can increase chances for such discoloration in the face.

Fluid retention is common in pregnancy, especially in the last trimester. The feet and the ankles may swell enough to warrant buying a larger pair of shoes. If you elevate your feet at regular intervals, do your ankle rotations, drink lots of water and avoid salty foods, you will have fewer problems with swelling, although it will not disappear. Do observe good sitting posture and avoid staying in one position for a long time. Do not sit with your knees crossed. Instead, sit on the sitting bones with the knees far enough apart that the uterus can rest between the legs instead of on them. Sitting cross-legged on the floor some of the time is a good idea too.

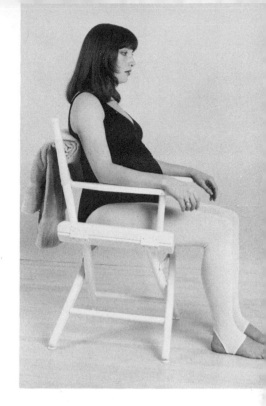

Fluid retention in the hands may make your rings too tight. Remove them before they are uncomfortable.

If you are prone to lower back aches, do at least 20 repetitions of the cat pose or do this exercise off and on through the day, especially before you go to bed at night. Upper back aches are almost as common in pregnancy. They often disappear once exercising has become a routine.

If you should experience any back pain, pay close attention to your posture during your daily activities—both your standing and your sitting posture. Use a foot stool off and on through the day. Place one foot on it while you stand and both feet when you sit. Always sit on the sitting bones rather than on the lower back. Try not to slump and lean your upper body on the lower part, because when the baby gets larger and the uterus expands up, you will be leaning on your uterus, compressing the liver and stomach.

Pain on the right side under the ribs—especially while seated—is a common complaint during the last trimester. If it occurs, make yourself sit up straighter. Hang a large towel over the back of the straight chair you use the most. Roll part of this towel up so the roll is just below your shoulder blades when you lean against the backrest, and fasten it in place. Notice how this reminds you to lift your upper body off the midriff.

Make it a habit to check your breathing regularly. And when you find yourself at a difficult task, remember to breathe easily with an even flow of air, using whatever type of breathing best fits the circumstances.

If exercise and diet do not prevent your waking up with painful leg cramps ask your partner to help you ease the pain. Place your foot in his hand and ask him to press the toes toward you while his other hand firmly massages the painful calf. Keep your knee straight.

Some women experience pain radiating from the lower back through the buttocks to the legs as a result of a pinched sciatic nerve. During an acute attack keep the area warm, rest and eat foods you digest well. When

most of the pain is gone, stretch the region under stress gently every day. Lie on your back with one knee bent. Raise your other leg straight up. Keep the buttocks pressed into the floor, the knee straight and flex the toes toward you. Place both hands on the straight knee and pull the leg gently closer to your body. Hold it at the point of maximum stretch.

A massage, an acupressure treatment or an adjustment of the spine by a chiropractor often helps the body overcome these common aches and pains caused by nerve pressure or muscle spasm. But before you see such a paraprofessional health expert, check with your physician to make sure your complaint is not the kind that needs medical attention.

You will probably find that your second and subsequent pregnancies are quite different from the first. Not only may the romance and novelty be gone, but you may have—if your pregnancy followed the first one closely—a small child to care for, leaving you little time to yourself. And you may worry about the child's responses to the new baby and about having enough love for two. Keep in mind that love is not a commodity; it does not diminish as it is given; it increases. I think it's best not to over-prepare a small child—who really can't yet understand about the sharing it will have to do—rather talk about the baby inside you and how it will one day come out and be part of the family.

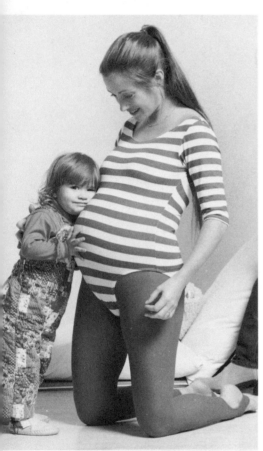

Avoid lifting your child whenever possible; squat down to hug and talk to it instead. Second and subsequent pregnancies are often physically different from the first, and they can be slightly more uncomfortable. The abdomen usually bulges out sooner, the baby seems lower and the uterine contractions of pregnancy may be noticed earlier and may be stronger and more frequent, making you believe that the baby will come early. Yet a pre-labor pelvic examination usually reveals that even though you feel you're carrying the baby lower, it has not yet entered the birth canal. A second baby often doesn't drop into this passage until the strong contractions of labor begin. This—in spite of your symptoms and wishful thinking—will probably not be much before the predicted due date. If you had a difficult or long labor with your first child it does not necessarily mean it will happen again, so don't anticipate problems and do what you can to make this experience special in its own way.

THOSE VERY LAST WEEKS

During the last weeks of pregnancy a woman's eating and sleeping patterns change. Large meals can't be managed because the stomach is left so little space. Nibbling on healthy foods, those which experience has taught you cause the least amount of heartburn, now works better. A straight eight-hour sleep also seems to be a thing of the past.

Sometimes restlessness at night can be eased when the schedule in the day is less hectic, sometimes sleep is deeper after a bedtime snack—perhaps an easily digestible protein such as cottage cheese or yogurt, or a peanut butter and jam sandwich on whole wheat bread and some fresh fruit. The uterus will now be pressing on the bladder too, and you may have to make a few trips to the bathroom during the night. Once awake, it is sometimes difficult to get back to sleep. So make the bed comfortable with a backrest and pillows. This may not leave enough space for two, but a bed all to yourself leaves you free to toss and turn. And if your partner is allowed uninterrupted sleep, there won't be two cranky people living together. The partner of a woman about to give birth needs all the rest he can get, because those last days are difficult for an expectant mother. Your labor may start at any time and can last a long time and you will need a well-rested coach. If you have difficulty sleeping, try to take naps in the daytime. Sleep when you can and don't worry about it when you can't. Learn to pay attention to your body's cycles rather than to the clock and you'll be better prepared to mother your infant.

Should you go past your due date you may become seized by the irrational fear that you will be pregnant forever. Some women find themselves depressed at this point—especially those who have interrupted their careers. Keep doing things which interest you. A demure lady-in-waiting may look lovely in a photograph, but passive waiting rarely brings any kind of fulfillment in real life. Also be aware that your due date is only an approximation. If the baby arrives two weeks ahead of schedule it is not considered early, nor is it late when it waits till two weeks past the due date.

At times the general discomfort of those very last weeks may well seem overwhelming. Try to focus inward to see the completely formed little being who is eating and sleeping and moving about and probably starting a thought process all its own. I never cease to be awed when I think how a woman's body can allow a new life to form and deliver it into the world.

If the thought that the virgin-like beauty of your body is gone and may never completely return threatens you, take a good look at nature. Notice how there is beauty to every stage of life. Look at the trees. The ones which inspire us most are not the straight-boled young ones but those whose trunks reveal that they have held their own through many storms. The same is true for you. A special beauty accompanies every fully lived stage of life.

Part Two

Preparing for Labor & Birth

PREPARING YOURSELF

During the last weeks of pregnancy, the body, ripe with the promise it holds, is a constant reminder of the process about to begin. Expectant mothers wonder how it will happen. "Will I be able to handle my labor? What will it be like? How does it hurt? Will it cause damage? Will he be there when I need him? Will he help me?" The baby becomes almost secondary. It will regain its status once labor is over. Now the mother thinks of herself, but her wellbeing and that of her baby are so closely intertwined that this usually serves her baby best too.

When you think of labor you will probably be torn between feelings of fear and hope. They are strong emotions; allow both to surface and use this energy to practice the self-discipline you have learned.

Even with an excellent coach, giving birth remains a woman's labor. The major part of the work is yours and so is the major part of the preparation. Practice your pregnancy exercises with increasing attention to detail. Move slowly and gracefully. Place the body correctly and then work. Pay attention both to posture and to the exercise itself. Feel the muscles involved in each exercise contract and relax, and use others only to maintain good posture. Allow for slight position changes to avoid muscle strain.

Your breathing muscles are the most crucial ones to learn to control, because breathing plays such a large part in controlling your response to work, stress and pain.

During labor, the cervix stretches open over the baby's head, as does the birth passage. This stretching will encounter the least resistance when the surrounding muscles are relaxed, because of the way voluntary and involuntary muscles affect each other. When the sensation of stretching intensifies, it changes to pain and you may be tempted to tighten your muscles and hold your breath.

You will not be able to consciously control the duration of a labor contraction, and halfway through the contraction, you may think, "I don't want to do this." You will need to try to overcome the temptation to fight the rest of the contraction—fighting will make it hurt more, tire you more and there will be less progress. Your practicing will enable you to take control of your breathing muscles first, continue to let them work, then allow that control to spread, first to the pelvic area, then to all other voluntary muscles.

When you are doing your Pregnancy Workout watch your breathing. If a particular exercise hinders deep breathing, breathe faster and less deeply, using the rib cage more and the abdomen less. Switch to panting and learn to pant without strain. When pain triggers a tightening reaction, it does so in every muscle, including those used in breathing. That's why holding one's breath is a common reaction to pain. But the air you breathe is the fuel for muscle work and your uterus will work better when it is given oxygen and allowed to pass off its waste.

Muscles which tighten use energy, and energy during labor is precious. If you have become used to consciously tensing and relaxing muscles during an exercise session, you will have built stronger connections from the brain to different muscle groups, increasing your control over their response, including their response to labor.

Pay attention to your stretches. Do them at different times during the day. Avoid clothes which restrict you—they can inhibit proper posture. Do not sag, slump or strain. When your body seems to want to fight a stretch, make sure your position is correct so the stretch is where it is meant to be. Then use your breathing to control the impulse to tighten or to stop. Keep it even and easy. Change to light panting. Concentrate on your breathing and enjoy the stretching sensation. Time yourself by counting and try to hold each stretch a half-second longer every time.

As you do your exercises during those last weeks of pregnancy it is important to wait until you have completed a stretch, then move back to a centered position and take a few deep breaths. Move on to the next exercise only when the strain from the one before is gone. This will help to remind you, in labor, to regain your composure after each contraction, then to rest and gather strength for the next one.

Complete every exercise session with a few minutes of deep relaxation. Here, too, position the body correctly and support yourself with pillows. Do not repress your thoughts and feelings; pay attention to them. Follow up on them when necessary, otherwise let it pass. Let outside noises and little desires for this and for that drift by. They cause but a surface stirring. Let fears and hopes and expectations well up. They are just a rippling in an unfathomable process.

Without straining, focus on your breathing. Open your body to the air when it comes in. Let tension flow out as you exhale. Your body will become more receptive with each inhalation, and with each exhalation there is less tension. This is how you will try to handle labor, your body relaxed and your mind, aware of pain and desire but not at their mercy, focused on simply allowing the process of birth to take place.

HAVING A COACH DURING LABOR

For the past ten years I have taught my birth preparation course at the same hospital where I worked as a labor and delivery nurse. One night the labor of a young woman began during class. When her contractions got stronger, she went up to the labor and delivery department. I promised to come up after class to help her. She was married to a young man from Israel, and it was their first child. They were pious Jews with an orthodox faith. Because of their religion, he could not touch her during labor and he could not see the birth. The affinity between them was clearly perceptible in the labor room. She sometimes seemed to care more about his agony of not being able to hold her than about her pain. In the delivery room, he placed himself so he could not see her. A strong expulsive contraction made her cry out. His reading from the prayer book became louder and faster. Silence followed, then her voice, this time high with excitement, exclaimed: "A girl, oh a girl, a beautiful girl." He bowed his head in reverence.

It was only very recently in our culture that it became popular for a father to assist at his child's birth, and many men are still not comfortable with it. It can be very painful for a woman if her partner is unwilling to coach her, especially if she wants him to show his interest in being a father through the role of coach. She understands that birth is not just the culmination of her pregnancy, but the beginning of a new life, and she wants her partner to be as involved as he can, because the contribution a man can make during his baby's birth is much more than that of coach. It can become a time of great emotional and spiritual union, a real beginning for the new family. Coaching becomes the concrete expression of the father's commitment to this family.

But when it becomes clear that her partner cannot be her coach, a wise woman will ask someone else to help her, and let her partner express his commitment in his own way.

I don't know from personal experience what it is like to be coached through labor, but I know from watching couples and single women who brought someone to help them that the skills of coaching are the same whether the partner is a nurse, a midwife, a doctor, a friend or the child's father. Of course between lovers the interaction has a chemistry all its own, and may make a woman incredibly relaxed, almost serene, throughout labor and birth. Yet a single woman can have an experience as rich in its own way when she has a coach who is warm and caring.

A man is able to coach a woman through labor in the same way that someone who is paralyzed can coach a basketball team. He will need a thorough understanding of the rules of the game and a knowledge of how to play it, but the ability to play himself is not a prerequisite.

In the pages to follow it is sometimes necessary for the sake of clarity to refer to the coach with the words "he," "his," "him." Please understand this is meant to distinguish the coach from the mother, whether the coach is a woman or a man.

FOR THE COACH:

As her coach, you help a woman bridge the gap between practice sessions and the realities of labor. If she has learned to relax to your touch and to listen to your suggestions about handling contractions, then your touch, voice and suggestions become her focus and with them you help her through waves of labor which might otherwise seem overwhelming. It will take practice for the two of you to establish this interaction. It is difficult to predict how much practice you will need—it partly depends on whether some of these skills are already familiar to both of you.

RELAXATION PRACTICE

When you talk to your partner as you coach her in relaxation techniques, allow your voice to be gentle so as to enhance her ability to concentrate on herself. This is not the time to ask for attention—simply give her your attention. Relax yourself before you start. If you do not know how, let her teach you—you might do the exercises along with her. Your own body will relax better after it has been worked and stretched, and your practice sessions together will have a spirit of mutual commitment.

The first time you work on relaxation together, the mother-to-be should be in a semi-sitting rather than a side-lying position to make her responses easier to check. Correct positioning is important during practice, but crucial during labor. For practice use a comfortable lounge chair, a backrest, a tipped-over chair, or a board with pillows. The woman should lift each buttock up and back to make sure she is properly based. Then ask her to lean back. The edge of her buttocks and lower back should be against the backrest where it leaves the bed or the floor. The back should be supported so it rises in a straight line up from the pelvis. Place a large firm pillow under the thighs to help the hip muscles relax and a smaller one under the head so it is slightly tilted forward. You can support the arms with pillows as well if you wish.

Realize that tension can be contagious. If you are tense, she will be. Don't rush along. Place yourself so that you can touch her hips and legs

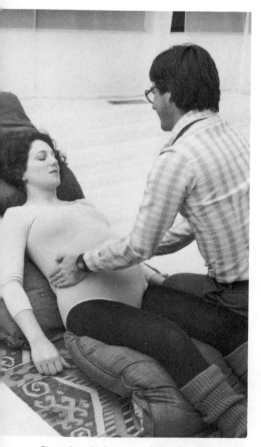

Gently slide your hands upwards a few times where her waist used to be . . .

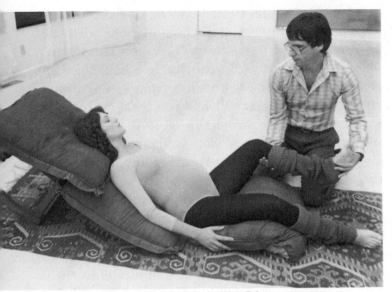

Lift this leg and rotate it in the hip . . .

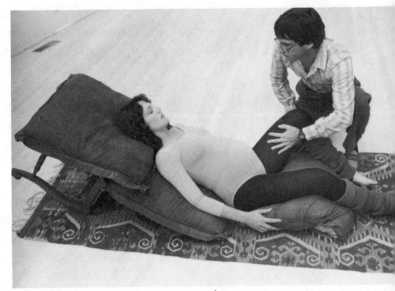

Have her push against your resistance . . .

without straining your back, arms or hands. Kneeling works best for me if the person I am working on is on a large bed or the floor. Suggest that she close her eyes and breathe slowly and deeply. Place your hands on her hips and gently slide your hands upwards a few times where her waist used to be. Ask her to take your hands and guide them exactly the way she would like them to go. During labor it helps to massage these large and sensitive muscles when a strong contraction makes her back arch or after a contraction when she is unable to relax. Next, slide your hands without touching the uterus along the front of the hips, down the lower abdomen to the inner thighs. Gently stroke or knead the muscles there a few times. Now place both hands on the same leg and slide them down to the knee. Let one stay behind the knee and slide the other farther down to place it behind the ankle. Lift this leg and rotate it in the hip smoothly and without jerking movements, letting the knee bend and straighten.

The leg should feel heavy in your hands yet it should rotate without resistance. If it does not, her leg muscles are not relaxed. Ordering her to "relax" will not help. Instead, put the leg down and ask her to tighten it as tight as she can. Then stroke it and ask her to relax it again. Repeat this a few times and observe together the difference between tension and relaxation. Then have her bend the knee slightly. Place your hand just above the knee on the outer thigh. Ask her to push your hand away with her leg. Resist her pushing. Place your hand on the inner thigh just above the knee and have her again push against your resistance. The voluntary tensing of a muscle often increases one's ability to relax it. Let her leg rest on the pillow once more, and firmly knead the very upper part of the leg right at the hip joint. Check the leg again to see if it rotates more smoothly. Then work on the other leg in a similar fashion.

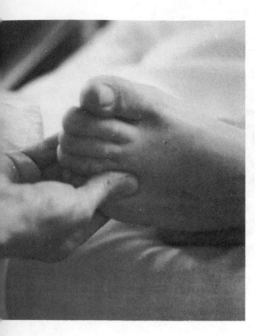

Place your hands on the soles of her feet with your thumbs at the junction of the two outer toes. Now make small circular motions with the thumbs, applying slight pressure right where the two smallest toes merge, then at the junction of the second and third toes. After you have touched every toe junction, place your hands on her feet in such a way that you can put slight pressure on the outside of the small toe. Ask her to relax her feet into your hands. Suggest that she picture a path of relaxation which winds from your fingers through her feet, ankles, calves, thighs, hips, buttocks, and lower abdomen. It is in this area that learning to relax is most important because during labor it is here that the temptation to tighten in response to the pain will be greatest, and it is in these muscles that such tightening may impede the progress of labor.

In between labor contractions a foot massage can be quite helpful. First firmly massage the soles of her feet with the ball of the thumb or the palm of one hand while your other hand holds the toes and stretches them forward. Then let your fingers stroke and apply pressure where it helps her relax. Sensitive areas are the outside of the little toes, the inside of the foot where the heel rises out of the arch, and the ankle behind and below the protruding ankle bones. A Shiatsu technique (Japanese acupressure) during a contraction is to rub the muscles over the hips, then the outer little toes at their junction with the foot.

Look at her body from the waist down. The abdomen moves with her breath. Her legs are turned out a bit at the hips to reveal the inner thighs; they are bent at the knees. When you touch the buttocks or thighs your hands should feel no tension. If they do, work on that area a little more next time.

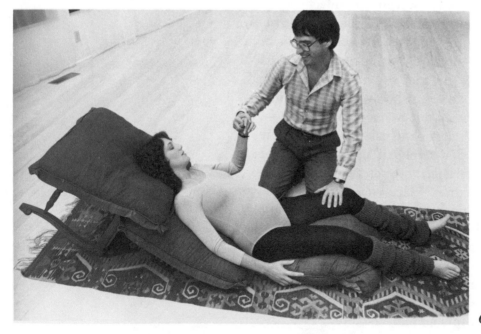

Check her arms for relaxation . . .

The neck and shoulder area is the next important region to learn to relax, because tension here will get in the way of proper breathing. Kneel next to her in such a way that you can touch the tops of both shoulders. Knead them from the outer edge to her neck and back a few times, then slide your hands behind her shoulders to knead the muscles there. Next slide them to the front till you reach the large muscles above the breasts which connect the front of her arm with her chest. Work this muscle on each side. Slide your hands to the upper shoulders again and rest them there to look at her for a moment. Her body should be supported in such a way that her chest opens when her shoulders relax. If you notice that the shoulders are pushed forward, place a small pillow or folded towel between the shoulder blades. Now check her arms for relaxation. Both should bend easily at the elbows and rotate smoothly at the shoulders. If the arms are not relaxed, help her find the difference between tensing and releasing in the same way you did with the legs, first by watching her tighten and relax a few times to your commands, then by having her work against resistance, like this: Have her lift one arm, elbow bent. Place your hand inside the forearm and ask her to bring the arm in. Resist her effort. Place your hand on the outside of her forearm and ask her to push the arm out. Resist this movement. Then have her pull on your hand. Finally, knead the upper arm right at the shoulder joint, then slide both hands down the arm, past the wrist, and lift it up by the hand and place it on a large pillow. Do the same with the other arm and hand.

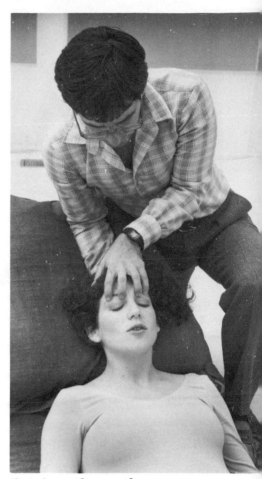

Continue the gentle pressure on the edges of the skull and the eye sockets . . .

You should concentrate finally on relaxing the area of her neck where it meets her head, skull, and face. Slide your fingers behind her neck where it rises out of the shoulders and feel for the large vertebra there. Slide the fingertips to each side of this knob and with gentle rotating movements move up along the neck over the muscle ridges along each side of the cervical vertebrae until your fingers bump into the skull line. Apply gentle pressure on this bony ridge with one hand. Place two fingers of your other hand on each side of her nose on the bony ridge behind her eyebrows. Pause here for a few moments. Slight pressure simultaneously applied on these ridges releases tension in the skull which helps in turn to relax other areas in the body as well. Continue the gentle pressure on the edges of the skull and the eye sockets with your hands relaxed, and suggest that she concentrate on the pelvic region. This is where most pregnant women become very tired. Ask her to release tension in the pelvic area starting at the lower back and circling around the hip bones to the middle of the pubic bone. Suggest that she relax her legs in the hip sockets. Then ask her to focus her attention first on the tailbone, then slowly up along the spine, one vertebra at a time, to relax the muscles along the spine. Mention in slow succession the lower back, the waist, the area in between the shoulders and where the neck enters the head. Gently take your hands away. Place your thumbs so they meet in the middle of her forehead and stroke the forehead a few times. Then place your fingers at her temples

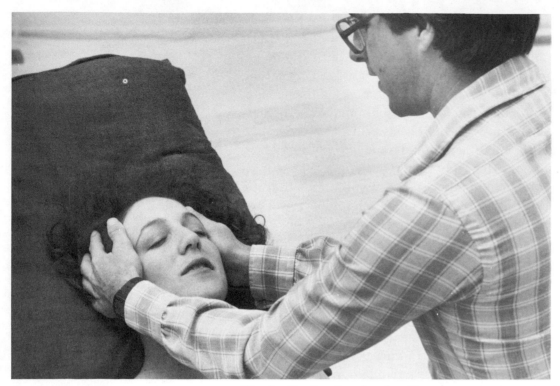

Stroke the forehead a few times . . .

and make a few small rotations here. Slide your fingers down to where the jaws meet and make a few rotations there. Stroke with your thumbs from the base of her nose and the corners of the mouth over the cheeks to the ears. Place your fingers behind her ears, slide your thumbs over the front of her ears and pull the ears gently out and up, then down. Slide your fingers through her hair and gently roll her head from side to side.

When she is fully relaxed, you are ready to combine this deep relaxation with the breathing techniques for labor. If the result of this first practice session was not too satisfying, try it again—it sometimes takes several times. Your skill in helping her release tension will be crucial during labor, so keep practicing, but do not attempt to give a formal massage. Instead, use your knowledge of her—any of the secret strokes which you know help to ease her tension. Be aware that in some women the need to be graceful is so strong that they cannot let their legs be heavy in another's hands. If your partner has this difficulty, encourage her as best you can, with reassurances or some good-natured humor.

THE BIRTH PROCESS: WHAT WILL HAPPEN?

While you are practicing these basic relaxation techniques together, both mother-to-be and coach should learn about the birth process itself. At first glance the mechanism of labor appears quite simple. The uterus contracts intermittently. During a contraction the uterus becomes shorter, thus it protrudes and compresses its content. Pressure on the cervix results. The cervix responds by retracting; it is first pulled up, then open. The pulling up is called effacement, the opening up dilatation. Effacement is measured in percentages; dilatation in centimeters. When the cervix is fully open around the baby's head (in medical terminology this is called 100 percent effaced and 10 centimeters dilated), the shortening or contracting of the uterus which continues at regular intervals pushes the baby out through the birth canal.

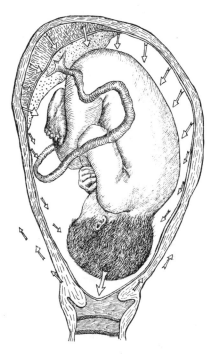

A UTERINE CONTRACTION, CERVIX FULLY EFFACED AND APPROXIMATELY 5 CM DILATED

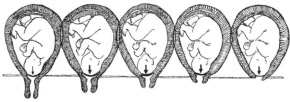

Effacement from 0 to 100 percent

Dilatation from fingertip to 10 centimeters

Most babies travel the short journey down the birth passage head first. They enter this passage facing one or the other of the mother's hips (because a baby's head is largest from front to back and the pelvis near the entrance is widest from side to side). The widest part at the entrance to the birth passage is called minus-five station. The point at which the baby begins to turn its head sideways to fit the passage is measured as minus-three station. Below minus-three station, the passage begins to curve toward the back to move around the pubic bone. During the descent brought about by dilation contractions the diameter slowly changes, becoming narrower sideways and wider from front to back, and the point where this change is most noticeable is zero station. The pressure of the dilation contractions usually moves the baby this far down. The baby's

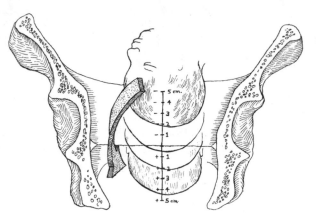

Turning past the stations

head adjusts to the changing shape of the passage into which it is pushed by pulling its chin onto its chest and turning the face toward its mother's back. Now the crown of the head can pivot down to get around the pubic bone. At plus-one station, it is so deep in its mother's pelvis that the resulting pressure there triggers her bearing-down reflex. If her cervix is fully open, she can follow this urge to push and time her efforts with the contractions. Now the crown of the baby's head pivots up toward the opening of the vagina. At plus-five station, the emerging head has stretched this exit wide open. Upon release from the passage, the head returns to the sideways position. The shoulders line up, they exit, then quickly the slippery baby is born. Contractions continue and the walls of the now empty uterus shorten, first detaching and expelling the placenta, then compressing the vessels which carried nourishment and waste mate-

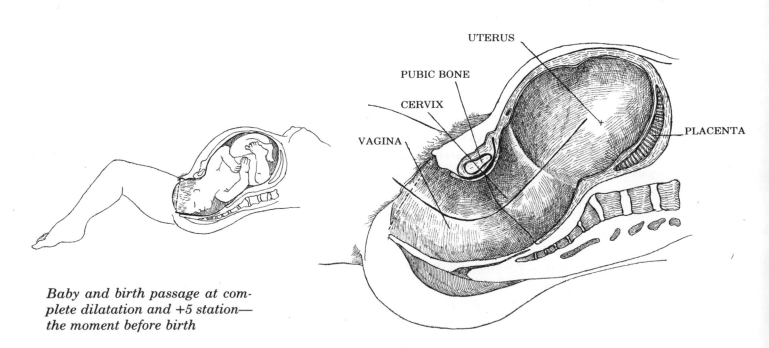

Baby and birth passage at complete dilatation and +5 station—the moment before birth

rials to and from the baby. These healing contractions will strengthen when the infant is put to the breast because the hormone that releases the breast fluid during suckling is also the one which makes the uterus contract.

In this elegant process, nature reveals her precision in all the infinite variations which take place. The slightest change has an effect, and it is impossible for us, with our human limitations, to summarize or account with any certainty for the seemingly infinite variety of experiences in childbirth. Don't be frustrated if your labor is different from what you expected, and don't try to convince yourself that you can control the process. Instead, accept fully the fact that you are in labor and that this work has to be done; then do it to the best of your ability. Try to enjoy the great beauty of being part of nature at work. Childbirth is a matter of accepting and working with reality, not with preconceived notions. By practicing with your partner to work together to facilitate the birth process, you cannot eliminate the possibility of a narrow pelvis, of a cord wrapped around the baby, or of a placenta which causes trouble. What you ensure is not that no problem will occur, but that whether it does or does not, you will be able to respond to the best of your ability.

DEALING WITH PAIN

It is not abnormal for labor to hurt. Any sensation, including pressure and stretching, changes into pain when it becomes too strong. The amount of pain you feel is first and foremost affected by your physiology. If the birth passage is spacious, if the cervix opens easily and if the surrounding muscles stretch well, it will hurt less. Pain is affected too by your state of mind. A woman who understands the process of labor, who is prepared to work with her contractions, who feels well cared for and is well rested, will be able to cooperate and raise her tolerance for what she might otherwise have interpreted as unbearable pain. And it has been observed that a woman who has learned to concentrate deeply on cooperating with her body, on controlled breathing and relaxation, may by such concentration actually be able to raise her threshold of pain. Your mind can be helped to perceive one stimulus less by focusing it on another.

But even under optimal conditions the birth process is often reported as painful, reminding us that living seems a process of mind *with* rather than mind *over* matter.

Once labor begins to hurt (and this may be at one centimeter dilatation or at five) a woman becomes increasingly sensitive to the sincerity of everyone around her. She wants people who care. Your partner's involvement will be a great asset to you, but he will have to overcome his impulse to shelter and protect you. He can't take the pain away, but he can help you handle it.

Every adult has had to face pain of some kind, despite our advanced medical and pharmaceutical technology. We all have to learn to deal with it. Ideally the woman in labor will not fear something is wrong; she will be confident that it will eventually stop, and be able to deal with the inevitable. But pain attacks that confidence. Even a woman who had accepted that it would hurt and might last a long time begins to have doubts during labor. She thinks first that it hurts more than it should, therefore something is wrong, second that it will never end and third that she lacks the strength to continue. Here her coach comes in. He becomes her perspective, her reminder and her instructor: "Don't let the pain scare you. It is the cervix opening up and the baby coming down. Nothing is wrong. Pain is within the nature of birth. Each contraction brings you closer. Let's take one contraction at a time. Let me help you rest when one is over and let's handle the next one together."

Make sure you have worked out ahead of time any disagreement between the two of you over the use of drugs to relieve pain. A woman does not prove herself through a "natural" birth if this is equated with one free of drugs. Sure it is best to keep drugs to a minimum. But sometimes pain relief is essential for labor to progress. Sometimes it is necessary because a woman has reached her limit. Refusing relief under such circumstances is not natural; it is misinformed and primitive.

When you, as the mother-to-be, reflect on these things, let them reach the deeper, more inaccessible regions of your mind and pay attention to the responses which come back. Picture your inner life as a house with many rooms. The doors to these rooms open with love. With a baby inside you, there is more love in your life than before. Thus new doors open to reveal parts of yourself you did not know.

As a woman you are strong and capable of performing a tedious task because the task is there and has to be done. Birth is one of these tasks. When you find yourself fearful of pain, accept it. It would be strange if you did not feel it. Speak back to it, though. Tell yourself: "The pain of birth is different from all other pains. First because it is not a sign that something is wrong, but a sign that the body is doing what it needs to do. Thus it is the one pain I can truly relax into. Second, it is intermittent, so there is time to rest. Third, it *will* end, and end in a positive way. This pain will take me somewhere, it is preparing me for the wonderful high of holding my baby."

During hard labor you may not remember this. But your coach will remind you. Learn to respond to his voice and touch. Teach your partner how and where his touch helps you relax, and make corrections where necessary without putting him down.

Now for the coach's role: When you coach a woman through a difficult labor, thoughtfulness and the ability to give are essentials. You acquire those like any other skill—by wanting to learn, and by practice and with feedback from your teacher, who is also your partner.

Since the amount of pain, her response to it and the length of her labor remain unknown, be prepared for a difficult labor while hoping for one that is easy. As a coach, try to spot tension and discomfort before she complains. Then use your confident presence, your hands and your voice to help her make the necessary corrections. Don't get angry if at first she cannot respond. You are doing this practicing so that she can develop trust in your skills *before* she is in labor, because later on pain will take away her willingness to try new things and to listen to an inexperienced person.

PRACTICING BREATHING AND EXPULSION TECHNIQUES TOGETHER

Anyone who has suffered severe abdominal cramps knows that one's immediate reaction is to double up in tension and hold his breath. Labor contractions trigger a similar response. And a uterus contracting strongly can make it difficult to use the surrounding muscles—the ones normally involved in breathing. Breathing techniques for the dilatation stage of labor are designed to help a woman overcome that built-in tension reaction and to enable her to switch to different breathing muscles where necessary.

As the coach, you can learn to understand these techniques; practice first a complete breath, the breath which uses all the skeletal muscles for breathing properly. Recline against a backrest or sit with the crown of your head lifted and the shoulders relaxed. Place one hand on your abdomen and one on your chest. Exhale. Now inhale slowly while expanding first the abdomen, then the chest, and finally the upper part of the chest at the neck and shoulders. Let the air flow out and increase this output by slowly lifting the abdomen in toward your back. Inhale again and slowly expand first the abdomen, then the chest and shoulders. Exhale and increase the exhalation by lifting your abdomen in. Watch your body move with the breathing and equalize the breath in and out by counting one, two, three, four in; one, two, three, four out.

Now watch your lady take a few complete breaths. Her full uterus will move out with her abdominal muscles, then her chest will expand. Halfway through an exhalation her bulging abdomen will lift inward and upward. During a labor contraction the uterus will rise outward and push down. Therefore an exhalation which contracts the abdominal muscles may interfere and be more uncomfortable.

So during a labor contraction the first departure from correct general breathing is to *totally relax the abdominal muscles during an exhala-*

tion. Try this with her a few times: Place both hands on her lower abdomen. Ask her to exhale, then inhale, expanding both abdomen and chest. When she exhales ask her to keep the lower abdominal muscles completely relaxed. Have her inhale again and watch her abdomen and chest expand slightly, and when she exhales ask her to concentrate on total relaxation of the lower abdominal muscles. Notice how this breathing is not quite as deep and therefore is slightly faster than the complete breath, and that her abdomen moves significantly less.

Later, in labor, during a strong contraction the mother may find even this slight movement difficult. She should be able to switch to a breathing which involves the abdomen even less by using the muscles in between the ribs. To learn how she will do this so-called slow chest breathing, each of you, mother and coach, should place both hands on your own rib cage with your fingertips touching in front and the thumbs pointing toward the back. Inhale by expanding the ribs, thus separating the fingertips. Exhale and allow them to touch again. Repeat a few times and make sure the breaths in and out are of equal duration. Notice how the abdomen still moves (because the diaphragm rises and falls with each breath) but less than with the slow deep breathing. The chest moves more. This breath is more superficial and therefore faster, so settle for a comfortable rate somewhere between 12 and 20 breaths per minute. Coach, when you watch your lady concentrate on this chest breathing, suggest to her the image of allowing her body to open up by relaxing it deeply from the waist down. Then check her legs at the hips for relaxation while she continues the steady chest breathing.

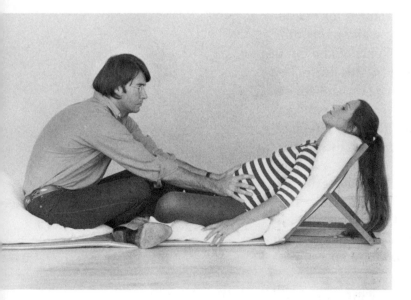
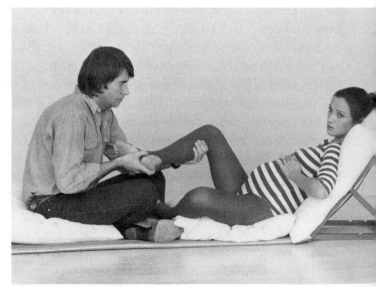

During labor, a very strong contraction is visible when a woman's abdomen is exposed. If you were to touch her belly you would feel the uterus become rock hard. At the peak of such a contraction even chest breathing can be too much movement. At that point she switches to panting. Both of you can practice this.

Panting produces less tension at the midriff when it is done through an open mouth, but this tends to make the throat dry. Use the following trick: Start with moist lips and a mouth rich in saliva. Relax the jaws so the mouth falls slightly open. Rest your moist tongue with its tip against or on the lower front teeth, allowing the middle part to curve up. Exhale audibly by giving the air a slight push. Let the air which rushes back in move over your moist tongue. Like wind over water it will pick up some moisture and prevent excessive dryness in the throat. Dip the tongue back in the saliva when necessary. Gently push the air out then let it rush back in and you'll discover that after a slightly forced exhalation the inhalation quietly takes care of itself. Your breath should be shallow and will therefore be rapid. Yet it appears effortless—a slight sound accompanies the air out, noiselessly it comes back in. The upper chest moves a little but the shoulders don't rock. The region of the midriff and the abdomen move too, but their movements are involuntary rather than intentional. The body is relaxed and still but for this gentle, light, rapid breath. Start with a rate of about 25 per minute, speed up to approximately one inhalation and exhalation per second, then slow down again. Learn to do this with such control that it produces no tension. Make sure that the breath in is equal to the one out in duration. Breathe slower and deeper as

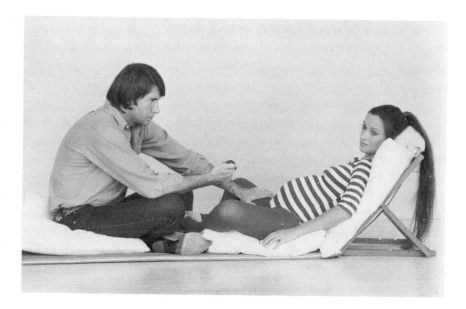

soon as you begin to feel you're not getting enough air, then gently speed up again and relax into your breathing knowing that you can breathe deeper whenever you need to.

Coach, when you turn to your lady to watch her do this panting, check her legs at the hips for relaxation again. Also, listen to her breath. The breath in is silent, the one out just audible, and silence and sound are of equal duration. It does sound like a child playing choo-choo trains.

It would be helpful if you could induce a few labor contractions just for practice, but instead you will have to pretend and imagine what labor will be like, so let me suggest how to proceed. As a coach announce, "Contraction begins," then both of you act as if it is true. Make up contractions of different duration, ranging in length from 45 to 90 seconds.

Now, for the mother-to-be: Take in a deep breath slowly and let your body expand. Exhale; let tension flow out with the air. Keep the lower abdominal muscles relaxed and check buttocks and thighs for relaxation. This cleansing breath is your message to yourself: "Time to work, to concentrate on cooperating with this contraction." Focus your eyes on some spot ahead and with your visual input thus limited, turn your mind inward. Picture the contraction. The uterus, as it shortens, rises outward and presses the baby on the cervix and into the birth passage. The sensations of pressure, pulling and stretching may merge into pain deep down inside. Overcome your natural reaction to pain by concentrating totally on breathing easily and on releasing every bit of tension wherever it arises. Breathe slowly and deeply when possible. Deep breathing gives the most energy for the least amount of effort. Allow your body to move with the breath. Expand it when you inhale and keep the lower abdomen slightly expanded with an exhalation. Picture a strong contraction which makes deep breathing difficult and switch to chest breathing, then to panting. Switch back to chest breathing and return to deep breathing as soon as your imaginary contraction allows. And when your coach says, "It is over," breathe a deep deep sigh of relief as if to say, "One less to go, time to rest."

As a coach, you can help the mother-to-be with the seeming infinity of 45 to 90 seconds of pain and hard work by breaking the time up into more manageable intervals: tell her when 15 seconds have passed, 30, 45, 60, and so forth. Pay attention to her as well as your watch. She can choose which breathing to do. You help her do it correctly. This means all breaths in and out should take equal amounts of time; the air moves constantly, it is never held; and the breathing is not done in such a way that it makes her tense. She should not pant too fast and she can swallow or burp as she needs to rather than repressing these functions and causing tension. She should start and finish with a deep breath. Practice making corrections in her breathing verbally, but it is even more important to correct her by example. During labor your being able to show her how to breathe can be of greater help than telling her. Many men say that during a hard contraction their wives focused on their eyes and, with their faces fairly close, they did the breathing with them. While you call off the time intervals and watch her breathing, keep an eye on her body for tension. Touch with relaxed hands where you see her tighten to help her let that tension go. Also, practice using your words to suggest how to get through the contraction. Try it first for a 60-second contraction. For example, you might say something like this:

"Take a deep breath in, let it out and focus. Concentrate on your breathing, keep your hips relaxed and your buttocks, relax your shoulders. Fifteen seconds over; don't let it frighten you; I can see it hurts. Don't arch your back, keep your thighs relaxed and the lower abdomen; it is half over. It will go down soon; try to breathe a little slower and deeper now, relax your jaws. The worst is over, relax into it now, 45 seconds over; a very nice job; we're almost there. Breathe slow and deep and begin to rest; take a deep breath and let it out; now rest until the next one." What is important about such a monologue is that it be sincere and relevant. It does not need to be original, entertaining or different with every contraction.

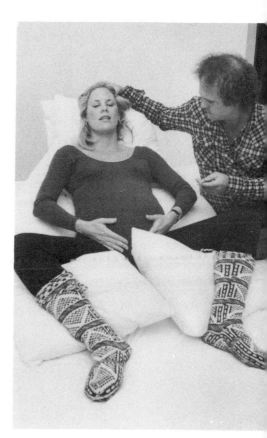

The arrival in the transitional phase between dilatation and expulsion is often marked by the sudden urge to bear down, and by long strong contractions, sometimes a full 90 seconds with less than a minute of rest between them. These contractions may leave a woman no time for a cleansing breath at the start. They grab her suddenly, then ease off only to build up once more. And the urge to bear down comes and goes. When an urge to bear down comes before the cervix is open, a woman keeps from giving in to this urge by blowing out little puffs of air right after she takes them in. Bearing down is done by taking in air, holding it and compressing it to increase the intra-abdominal pressure. Blowing does not eliminate the urge to push, it only keeps her from pushing at the wrong time. As soon as the urge subsides, it is better to return to breathing, since blowing increases chances for hyperventilation (breathing out more carbon dioxide than the body is able to produce, thus upsetting the balance between oxygen and carbon dioxide in the body). A disciplined, rhythmic pattern of breathing, something the body and mind count out like the rhythm of a catchy tune, helps many women overcome any panic response to these strong contractions.

Practice a few 90-second-long contractions. *As a coach,* spell out what such a contraction might be like. For example: "It starts, it is very strong, you have an urge to push, the urge is over, the contraction eases, it gets strong again, another urge to push, it is going away, the contraction is over."

You, as the mother-to-be, should respond to these imaginary transition contractions: take a quick cleansing breath, then rhythmically alternate panting and blowing in a pattern you like, for example, two crisp pants then blow, three pants then blow, four pants then blow; or just two pants then blow, repeated; or three pants and a blow, repeated. Choose a rhythm, then cling to the order this creates in the chaos of pain and fatigue. Breathe a little faster when the contraction is strong and slow down when it eases. Remember that hyperventilation is prevented by slowing your breathing a little and by allowing as much time for a breath in as for one out. Therefore in a pant-blow breathing pattern, make sure to take in a tiny bit of air before the little blow out. When you are imagining an urge to push, take some air in then blow it out, in-out, in-out, with relaxed lips and picture allowing the baby to stretch the birth passage open by keeping the buttocks, hip and lower abdominal muscles relaxed. Don't be afraid of the possibility that during actual labor in spite of your best efforts your body will give in to the pushing reflex. Nothing serious will happen. The reason for not bearing down before the cervix is open is that extra pressure on the cervix increases chances that it will swell up, thus slowing down dilatation. So you try to keep from bearing down not for fear of damage but for efficiency.

During these imaginary transition contractions, watch for tension, especially in the hips. During practice the mother should secretly tense different parts of her body to see if her coach notices this and can help her to relax.

When the cervix is fully open and expulsion begins, the uterus changes its function. From the baby's self-opening greenhouse it becomes its propeller. With each contraction it pushes the baby farther out of its mother's body. The mother changes her function too. From using all her control to lie back and not put tension on the uterus, she changes to real work. With each contraction she bears down with her uterus, keeping her birth passage relaxed.

The amount of effort it takes to deliver a baby from this point varies as much as the length of time and amount of pain involved in the opening up of the cervix. Some babies are out with the third contraction, others keep their mothers involved in strenuous pushing efforts for two hours.

Bearing down involves an interplay of many muscles. The muscles around the birth passage should be relaxed while the muscles of the abdomen should be contracted in a manner similar to that of a bowel movement but without tilting the pelvis or pulling the abdomen in. The breathing muscles are used to hold the breath. The muscles of the upper body are used to make the chest smaller, thus compressing the air and locking the diaphragm down to increase the intra-abdominal pressure. Finally the arm muscles increase the bearing-down force by gently pulling on the open legs, on the side rails of the bed or whatever is within comfortable reach.

The uterus contributes most of the pushing force, so you will push only during a contraction. With skillful efforts a woman can increase this force by one-third. A baby moves down the birth canal when pressure compels it. It stops coming down when the pressure lessens and it slips a little back up when the pressure altogether ceases. Therefore the greatest gain is made when a woman can push steadily and continuously for the duration of a contraction. Then she rests until the next one.

For a clear comprehension of the expulsive techniques, practice them step by step in the following manner:

Recline against a backrest at no more than a 45° angle. Pull the buttocks up and back, but don't arch or tilt the lower back; let it be well supported. Place your legs on those of your partner who is seated on a chair in between your open legs facing you. Put your hands on his ankles, which are placed on either side of your hips. Ask him to place a relaxed open hand on your lower abdomen over the edge of the pubic bone, with the thumb pointing to one side and the index finger to the other. Slowly push the abdomen out so it protrudes more, hold it out, and now smoothly and steadily push it straight down to the vagina. Your partner should see your abdomen move outward a little, then move down, and he should feel the muscles under his hand harden. Don't push hard, just steadily. Notice how the muscles in between the legs relax and bulge out when the abdominals bear down. This helpful reflex prevents you from tightening the area

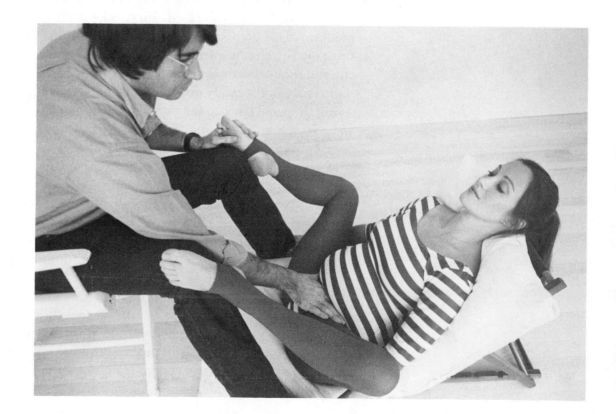

which needs to open during expulsive contractions. Relax a few moments, now bear down again. This time when you have the pressure right and your partner can feel the muscles harden under his hand, exhale somewhat forcefully and inhale quickly with an open mouth. During this exchange of air, try to keep the abdominal pressure on. Relax a few moments, then try again. Bear down by pushing the abdomen slightly out and steadily down. Then breathe out somewhat forcefully and quickly and in again. Ask your partner if you managed to continue to push during the air exchange.

If you did, combine the abdominal pressure with that of blocking and compressing air in the chest. First take a cleansing breath, then take a medium-sized breath and hold it. Block it in the chest and compress it by bringing the chin toward the chest and by bending the elbows up to round the shoulders downward and forward; then push the abdomen slightly out and gently but steadily down. Exhale with the chin still on the chest, then swing the head back to take with an open mouth a quick bite of air. Check with your partner if you managed to keep the abdominal pressure on. Continue to practice until you do.

Once you have mastered this control over the abdominal muscles during breathing, focus on relaxation of the hip muscles during the expulsive effort. After a quick cleansing breath, block a medium-sized breath in the chest, lean on it and push. Hold the pressure while your partner checks one then the other leg. Exchange the air quickly and efficiently as you need to. Your coach should place one hand under your ankle, the other under your knee and rotate your leg in the hip socket. It should move as easily as during the practice of relaxation.

After a few moments of rest finish by gently pulling on your partner's ankles while you inhale quickly, hold it, and bend your elbows up and forward. Now concentrate on pushing the baby into the vagina and on allowing the birth passage to open. Hold the air in as long as is comfortable, then exhale quickly and somewhat forcefully and swing the head back for a good bite of air. Watch your body work. There is some pressure at the throat but not much. The main pressure is in the chest as it locks the diaphragm down. The abdomen is pushing down and in response the muscles of the birth canal relax. The legs too are relaxed. But there will be some tension in the arms from their slight pull on your partner's ankles. The body remains supported by the backrest; only the head and the top of the shoulder come away from it.

Practicing this pushing will cause pressure on the baby, but don't worry, it won't come any sooner just because you pushed a few times. Don't push hard and don't practice lots of pushing contractions every day for weeks. Practice only enough to become thoroughly familiar with the techniques and every once in a while after that so as not to forget. While the baby will not come early from overzealous pushing practice, no one knows what such bearing down on a routine basis does to the ligaments which hold the uterus in place. Rest a few moments, then practice once more, this time with directions from your partner.

As the coach, you can help a woman with this discipline of bearing down, breath-holding and exchanging the air without letting go of the abdominal pressure, by knowing precisely what she is to do so you can give her directions and make corrections. Watch her closely so your instructions are in tune with her efforts. For some women the discipline of breath-holding is easier when the coach counts the seconds out. "Contraction begins, deep *breath in* and *out*. Medium *breath in, hold* it. *Block* it in the chest, *lean* on it and *push,* one, two, three, four, five, six, seven; exchange the air if you need to. Breathe out, in, hold, block, lean, push,

one, two . . . breathe out, in, hold, block, lean, push, one, two . . ." She pushes for the full length of a contraction and stops when it eases.

And finally time a few imaginary contractions lasting 60 to 90 seconds each. Check her technique while you give directions, then make the necessary corrections when you help her rest. Tell her, "Keep your chin close to the chest when you exhale, then swing your head back to inhale and make sure you take in enough air to help you push, but not so much that it makes you uncomfortable. Don't hold the air in for more than a count of ten and don't work too hard. Just steady smooth pressure will do it. Don't bring your whole body out of the backrest, only your head and shoulders. And don't pull too hard with your arms. Keep your legs as relaxed as possible. Try to keep the abdominal pressure on when you exchange the air. You don't need to get red in the face. Grunting noises will make your throat sore and they let some air out."

Some women say that they bear down better if they let the air slowly escape through somewhat pursed lips. Help her practice this method of breathing, and encourage her to try it during the expulsion stage of actual labor. If the baby comes down with this lesser effort she can continue to do it this way.

And finally, the mother-to-be can practice expulsion techniques for the delivery table in the following manner:

Lie down on the floor with two pillows under your head and shoulders. Place your legs on the seats of two identical chairs. Turn these chairs at such an angle that your hands fit on the front outer chair legs. The coach should kneel behind you and support you under the shoulders while he counts and gives directions. Keep both legs relaxed while tucking in the chin and rounding the shoulders to compress the air. You may be tempted to press them into the chairs (or stirrups) but this will cause tension in muscles which should be relaxed. Exchange the air quickly and efficiently while trying to keep the abdominal pressure on the baby, without making this a red-faced, all-out pushing effort. Steady and continuous pressure from the locked diaphragm and from the abdominal muscles with relaxation of the birth passage brings most babies down.

Now practice that very last expulsive contraction, the one during which the baby will be born. The birth attendant will ask you to bear down until

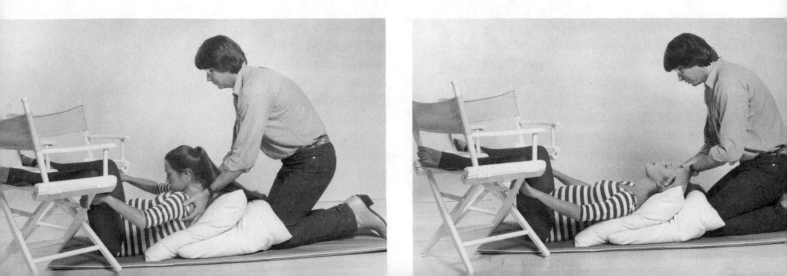

the full circumference of the baby's head has appeared, then she will say, "Stop pushing." With just the force of the uterus the baby's head will slide out. When the shoulders have lined up, you will be asked to bear down gently once more.

As her coach, you should pretend that you hear the doctor asking her to bear down steady and strong. Then suddenly he says, "Stop pushing." So interrupt your directions unexpectedly and lower her down in the pillows, telling her, "Blow, blow, blow; let the baby's head leave now; don't hold it back, but don't push either; blow, blow."

ABOUT PRACTICE—FOR MOTHER-TO-BE AND COACH

Evaluate together whether or not you and your coach need to review these skills to make them your own. If so, do set time aside to work on them so that one of you doesn't begin to feel resentful because the other doesn't seem dedicated enough.

Practicing to the point where the relaxation, breathing and expulsion techniques and the cooperation between you come easily will definitely be helpful. But there is no evidence that practice beyond that point is of much value—unless it eases tension or improves your relationship. Therefore allow the amount you practice to be a private matter between you, something you work out together.

When you have mastered the techniques, review them together in different positions for labor. Which position and what touches will be most helpful during labor will depend on where the woman feels the pain the most—deep down in the lower abdomen, in the lower back, or high up on the inner thighs. You won't know this until labor starts, but if you have practiced several positions you will be able to find the one most comfortable for you.

MAKING EARLY LABOR MORE COMFORTABLE

Early labor gets established better when a woman moves about in pleasant activities or sits upright. If a contraction overtakes you while standing or walking, place your legs a bit apart and bend the knees slightly. Place your hands on a table top, against the wall or on the shoulders of your

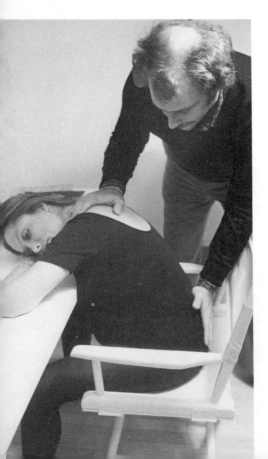

coach and lean the upper body slightly forward. Rock the pelvis if there is tension in the lower back. Your coach can place his arms around you with his hands against your lower back and your arms on his shoulders. He can rest his hands on your back or stroke your hips and buttocks. There is a spot on each side in the upper part of the buttocks which when pressed and rubbed helps a person relax the spine.

The semi-lotus position with the buttocks pulled back and the midriff lifted is another good position during early labor. If your back hurts, your coach can apply pressure. He should kneel behind you, place one hand against your lower back for pressure and the other on your shoulder for touch and support. He should not lean on your shoulder, but place his weight only on the hand which rubs the painful area of your lower back.

Sitting in a comfortable rocking chair might be fine for a while too. The rocking in between contractions helps relieve tension in the pelvic region. Tucking and releasing your pelvis a few times in between contractions is always a good idea. In early labor, many women find sitting on the toilet with the legs apart and the hands on the knees a helpful position, especially those who have to empty bladder and bowels frequently.

If you have strong back pain, a position in which the uterus can fall forward is often the most helpful. This can be done in a couple of ways: kneel on the floor in front of a chair with your arms on the chair seat and your legs slightly apart; sit at a kitchen or dining room table with your arms on the table top; or sit backwards on a chair with your arms on the back of the chair. Lean forward on your elbows, not by arching the upper back and thus compressing the diaphragm, but by bending from your hips with your legs well apart. In any sitting position, make it a habit to lift the buttocks up and back. There is less of a pull on the pelvis that way.

In the hospital, a woman can kneel in the bed with her arms on pillows on the raised side rails, or she can sit on a chair next to the bed with her arms on the bed. She can also still walk about if she prefers or if her labor is slowing down. When labor is felt primarily in the lower back the pain often does not go away when a contraction subsides.

As the coach, you will notice that in all these positions the woman's lower back is quite accessible to you. Counterpressure given with small rotations of a relaxed hand is very helpful in easing her back pain. Don't be afraid of pressing too hard. And stabilize her body against yours where necessary so she does not rock with the movement of your hand.

Applying heat with a hot-water bottle or heating pad to the lower back between contractions can help too. Some American Indian tribes used heated rocks, giving pressure and heat at the same time. During more advanced labor, quite a few women prefer a cold pack. Crushed ice in a plastic bag will do fine. Some alternate hot and cold. Such local use of hot and/or cold increases the circulation and thus helps to wash away the waste produced by tense muscles.

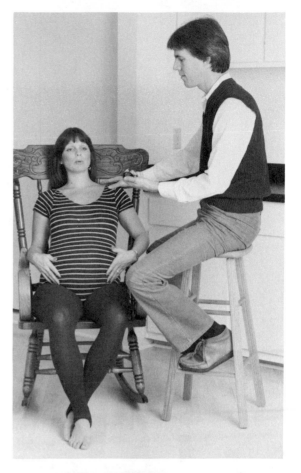

Positions for early labor

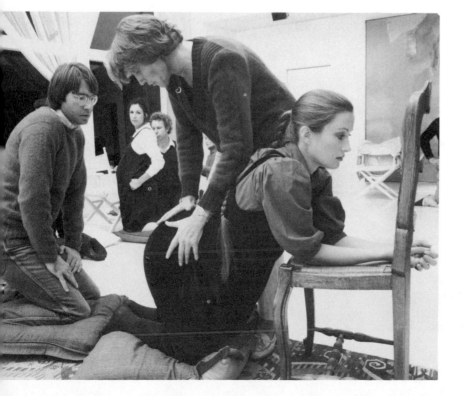

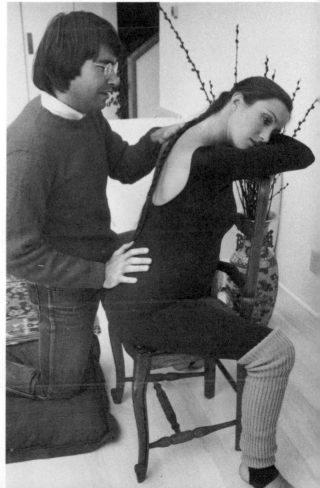

REHEARSING FOR ACTIVE LABOR

As labor progresses, most women become reluctant to move and they usually prefer a semi-reclining or side-lying position. But any position held for more than twenty minutes produces muscle strain. Therefore you as the coach should make slight changes by shifting the pillows, lowering or raising the backrest slightly, or by touching and rubbing the mother's shoulders and hips.

If she takes the reclining position, place a firm and large pillow under her thighs so her knees will be slightly bent and turned out, making the inner thighs somewhat visible. The body, including the lower back, should be well supported against the backrest and the chest should not be pushed forward.

In this position the expectant mother might like to stroke her own abdomen in this way: After taking a cleansing breath, place your hands on your pubic bone. As you inhale slide your hands with gentle pressure up through the groin, then with lighter touch along the hips to the top of the uterus; bring them in and, with the exhalation, slide them down over the middle of the abdomen with a very light stroke. With each breath the hands complete a circle. The faster the breathing, the faster the hands move. When a strong contraction makes panting necessary, keep the

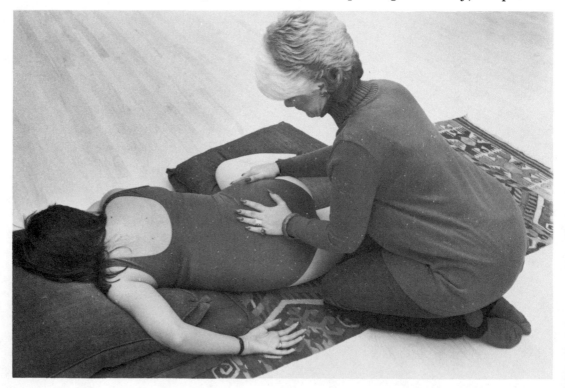

stroking to the groin area only. Move up and down in the groin with gentle pressure and relaxed fingers to relax the muscles there.

Some coaches place themselves in the labor bed, leaning against the back, the woman reclined against them between their open legs. They reach around her to give this gentle massage. It should be done in rhythm with her breathing and her hands should guide yours the first few strokes. It is quite a nice massage to give her those last days of pregnancy since the lower abdomen then can become painfully tired.

In the side-lying position her body should be well supported by pillows. If both her knees are bent equally, there should be a pillow in between them to help relax the upper hip. If her bottom leg is straight, the top one should be folded on a large firm pillow. Kneel behind her if she is on the floor. If she is on the bed, sit on the edge of the bed. Place the palm of the hand farthest away from her against her lower back and hold her upper hip with the other. Gently press with the palm of the hand against her lower back and rotate it in small circles. During labor, a woman can take quite a bit of pressure against her lower back. To give this without wearing out your hand and arm, shift the body weight into the massaging hand. Do not lean on or rub with the hand which holds her hip; this one is there to stabilize her when the pressure from the massaging hand increases. Learn to increase and decrease the amount of pressure against the back without tensing either hand. Ask her to place your hands exactly where she wants them. Make sure the supporting hand holds the hip about where the thigh leaves the body so that it does not touch the uterus.

As an expectant mother you may have heard that during expulsion quite a range of positions have been found to be helpful. Choose the one which gives you the least pain and the greatest sense of control. The pelvis is open wider when it is properly aligned and when the thighs are close to the body. This is why squatting is such an excellent position for a woman who is strong and flexible and not worn out by a long labor. Reclining with the legs open and pulled up close to the body can work well too. Don't sit up too high; it makes effective bearing down harder. Make sure the buttocks are pulled back so you can sit on the sitting bones, and don't arch or slump the lower back.

If you experience back pain during expulsion, a side-lying or kneeling position might be better. In the side-lying position, bring the open legs and the chin toward the chest. Ask your coach to apply counterpressure to the back and help you support the upper leg. Ask him not to pull this leg farther open than you place it. (If he did, your hip might hurt afterwards.)

In the kneeling position, keep your knees somewhat apart and put your arms on the shoulders of your coach—on his lap if he's sitting in a chair—or on the side rails of the bed. Bring your chin toward your chest and let your upper back round while your pelvis is neither released back nor tucked under. Just keep it relaxed and open. In this position the contractions often become stronger and come farther apart. Some women say bearing down is less painful when they kneel. If there is no progress in the baby's descent, try bearing down in another position.

In most hospitals the major part of bringing the baby down is done in the labor bed. In some the actual birth is allowed to take place in this

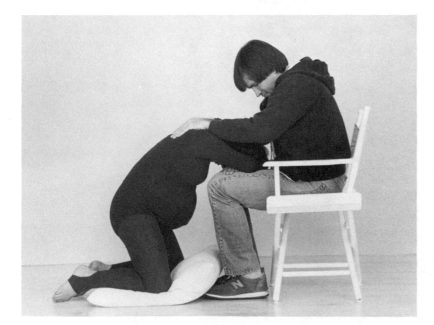

Positions for the expulsion stage

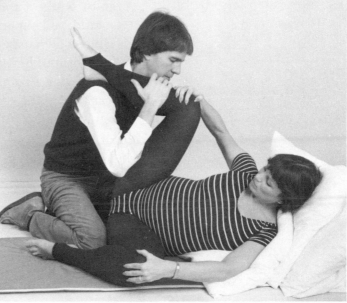

same bed, in whatever position the mother prefers. In some hospitals birth stools have been re-introduced. If you will be using one, practice bearing down seated in an armchair, your feet placed on footstools, your thighs up close to your body. Some women say that being seated in a birth stool is more comfortable than any other position during delivery, yet in medieval times midwives were accused of placing the mother on the stool too soon, thus wasting her strength and causing her unnecessary inconvenience.

Today this holds true for some obstetricians with regard to the delivery table. To be moved into the delivery room while the doctor is washing his hands and the nurse is getting the room ready is okay, but to be placed on this table with your buttocks right on the edge and your legs up in stirrups is not fair unless there is someone standing ready to catch the baby, who should be about to appear.

The back of this bedlike delivery-room table often cannot be raised. Two firm pillows under the head and shoulders will take away the helpless feeling of being flat on your back when everyone else is walking around. The table usually has handlebars on each side for gripping. If not, you can place your hands on the legs of the stirrups. These adjustable leg supporters should hold the legs comfortably: not too far apart and not too high or at unequal heights.

In the delivery room, your coach will be next to or behind you. The delivery room environment can be somewhat intimidating; your coach may have self-doubts. "The doctor and at least one nurse are there and what do you know?" he may ask himself. But he does know how to support you, and you have gotten used to his directions and voice. At the start of a contraction, take a cleansing breath. Your coach will suggest that you hold, then compress the next breath by tucking the chin in toward the chest while rounding the shoulders downward and forward. Your arms should pull slightly on the handlebars with your elbows bent up off the table. The hands of the coach should be under your shoulders to support you without lifting you higher. Such lifting will wear both of you out and it does not accomplish much at all. The coach can remind you to let your legs rest in the stirrups and to keep the buttocks relaxed. At the count of ten—or sooner if you need to—exhale in the curled-up position, then swing your head back to take, with an open mouth, a quick gulp of air. The coach should spice his directions and encouragement with praise to taste.

When the baby's head is out and has turned back to the sideways position, the shoulders have lined up. This usually happens in one contraction. If not, everyone, including the baby with just its head out, waits for the next contraction. When the mother feels the pressure from the shoulders mount, she takes some air in and pushes gently. Remind her to open her eyes because once the shoulders are out, the baby is out and you'll see that it looks larger right after birth than when it came sliding out. You could never put it back in.

Part Three

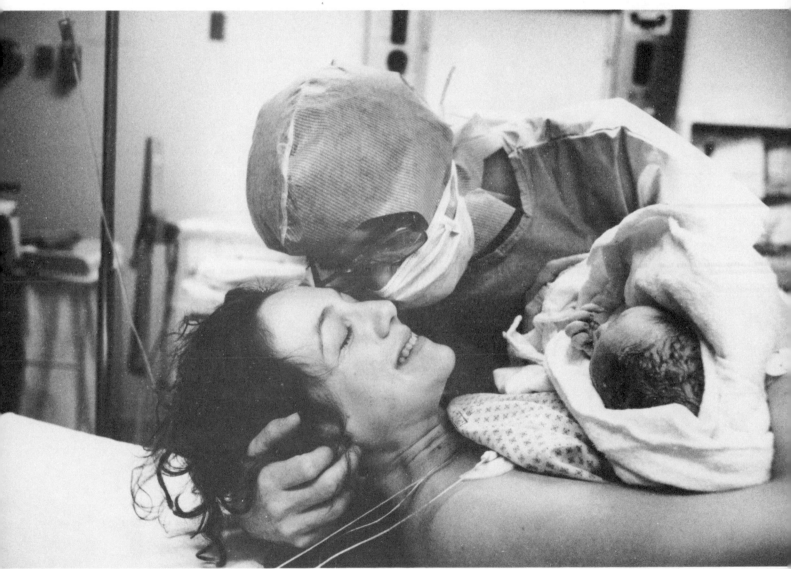

Labor & Birth

RECOGNIZING AND COPING WITH THE ONSET OF LABOR

For people who grew up in a culture which seems to function only with accurate measurements and exact schedules, where even vacations are planned with itineraries and maps, traveling through childbirth can be a trying experience. There are no road signs saying WATCH FOR THE ONSET OF LABOR, ENTERING ACTIVE LABOR, SWITCH TO PANTING BREATHING, or NEARING TRANSITION, WATCH FOR URGES TO PUSH. Without such posted signs, knowing where you are can be confusing and quite trying. You begin to understand how little the conscious mind is aware of the detailed workings of the body.

Even your doctor can have difficulty diagnosing the onset of labor. Labor is defined as a process of uterine contractions which continue on until the baby is born, thus setting labor apart from the contractions in pregnancy which come and go. But until about three centimeters dilatation, the uterus often takes its time and may even take a day or an afternoon off here and there. Contractions which stop before three centimeters dilatation are called pre-labor contractions. (They are also known by the confusing term of false labor or as Braxton Hicks contractions.) Those contractions which march right on into active labor are named early labor contractions. Often the difference between pre-labor and early labor can only be told in hindsight.

Just as a keen observer recognizes by changes in the sky that a thunderstorm is imminent, in the last weeks of pregnancy you can watch for those changes which will mark the transition from pre-labor to early labor. Some women notice this change in their physiology by a generalized sense of feeling unwell—as if something were wrong with dinner or they were coming down with the flu. Slight nausea, loose bowel movements, an ache in the lower back, or fluid loss through frequent urination are often reported. Others say they felt almost driven by a new energy. And there can be a change in the contractions. Those of pre-labor come and go. The uterus contracts from early pregnancy on. In most women these contractions become perceptible in the third trimester, and in quite a few they become so prominent as to be given the name "false labor." In some women they are bothersome, in others they are hardly noticed, and some never feel them at all. They may be more prominent after a busy day and they are usually not affected by a change in position. They may

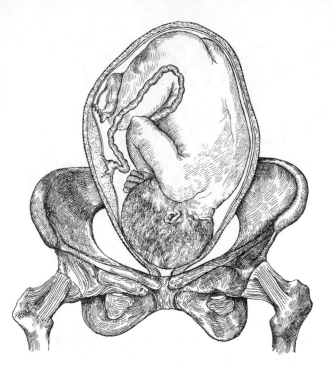

BABY AND MOTHER AT THE ONSET OF LABOR

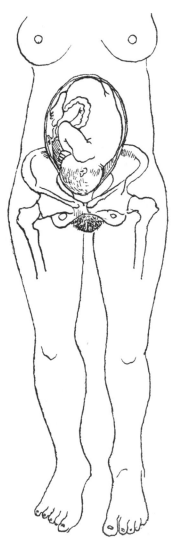

be uncomfortable but they can't be called painful. Their frequency, duration and intensity do not increase through time. Early labor contractions usually do accelerate. Thus when in doubt, time the length of your contractions and note the frequency with which they occur. When their length increases and the time in between them steadily decreases, it is probably real labor. Contractions which at first may have felt like a menstrual cramp feel different as labor becomes established. There is more energy involved, then there is pressure from the baby and possibly pain from the pull on the cervix. (A cervix which opens easily sometimes hurts less than one which resists; that is one of the reasons why early labor is painful for some and painless for others.) Early labor contractions are more often affected by a change in position. They might become more frequent during a walk, or become less perceptible when you are stretched out on your back (the position which makes it hardest for the uterus to function) and less frequent but stronger while kneeling or while lying on the left side. If early labor contractions bring about effacement and dilation they may dislodge the mucous plug. This mucus which solidified to seal off the cervix, will leave the vagina as a thick, usually somewhat pink discharge.

The progress from early labor to active labor is usually marked by a change in the pattern of the contractions. Generally they begin to last longer, come closer together and feel stronger. But occasionally, in a woman in whom early labor contractions came all night every three to five minutes, not painful but annoying enough to keep her awake, active labor will pull those contractions first farther apart, making them stronger, then, keeping them strong, will bring them closer together again.

Most women need contractions closer than five minutes apart, each lasting at least 45 to 60 seconds, to open the cervix more than three centimeters. But here again, there are exceptions. An occasional woman will progress past 3 cm with contractions 7 or 8 minutes apart. However, these are usually long, strong ones, the kind that make her change to panting breathing. Only a very rare woman will arrive in active labor without any recognizable signs. If the opening of the cervix did not cause perceptible contractions, there was probably the discharge of pink mucus from the vagina or the rupture of membranes to warn her.

A rupture of the membranes sometimes occurs unexpectedly before there are any signs of labor. Contact your physician if a sudden gush or a continuous leakage of water from the vagina occurs. If the rupture occurred prematurely, it might heal again with bed rest. Now cleanliness is very important. Nothing should enter the vagina. The amniotic fluid, which continues to be made and seep out after the initial rupture, is better caught with a sanitary napkin than with a tampon. Change this napkin often since warm moisture provides bacteria with an ideal feeding ground. Wash the area in between the legs regularly with a clean washcloth from the vagina forwards first, then from the vagina towards the back. At times rest with a clean towel under the buttocks and with the legs open to allow for circulation of air—most microorganisms which flourish in this region don't like air. A rupture in the membranes around the due date usually leads into labor. Because of the increased chance of infection and of prolapse of the cord, medical supervision is a must whenever membranes have ruptured.

Coaching a woman through birth is a form of loving. Working together often during those last days becomes an intimate exchange too. There is no medical reason why you should not make love, but you should abstain from the act of intercourse when the membranes have ruptured or the mucous plug has left the cervix because then mother and baby become more liable to infection.

During any Am-I-or-am-I-not-in-labor period, remember that digestion will probably slow down if labor progresses, so avoid heavy foods. If you aren't hungry, don't eat. If you are hungry, select foods which are digested easily: herb tea with honey, crackers or toast with jam, a bit of ripe fruit. Spend the time pleasantly. Take a shower, wash and set your hair, bake some favorite cookies, do some weeding in the garden or any other light physical activity. But should labor start at the end of a busy day, rest in a semi-reclining or side-lying position. Spend the time in between contractions pleasantly and during a contraction use whichever of the techniques you need. If your labor starts in the middle of the night and you can handle it alone do so to allow your partner some rest. After all it might stop again and come back the next night.

WHEN TO CONTACT PHYSICIAN OR MIDWIFE

Sometime during the third trimester discuss with your physician or midwife when he or she would like to be notified that labor may have started. When you time contractions, make two columns, one for start and one for finish. Your doctor will ask "how far apart are your contractions?" meaning, how much time elapses from the start of one to the start of the next.

Make a phone call immediately if:

- your physician desires to be called whenever there are signs of labor;
- there is a reason to believe that such a call will lessen your anxiety;
- the contraction pattern is such that you might be nearing active labor (3 cm dilatation)—these are contractions which are on the average five minutes apart and last more than 45 seconds, or contractions which are quite painful and long even though they are more than five minutes apart;
- the bag of water ruptures, releasing the sweet-smelling amniotic fluid, sometimes with a gush, sometimes with a trickle;
- there are signs of a complication (see page 142).

DEALING WITH THE HOSPITAL ENVIRONMENT AND STAFF

The feat of going to the medical center at the right time—not so early that you are sent home, not so late that you miss the onset of a problem or have the baby in the car—requires not only a solid understanding of the signs of progressing labor but excellent communication with your doctor and his staff.

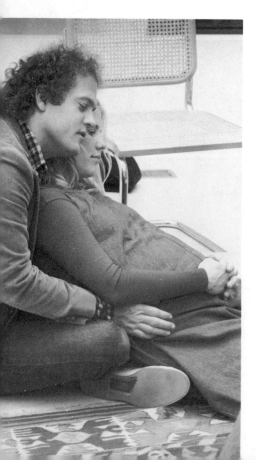

A doctor rarely comes to the home anymore. His or her skills have become part of a complex medical technology, and away from his equipment and staff, he loses many of the tools of his discipline. While going to a hospital (or perhaps more accurately, a medical center) for childbirth does have its problems, it also places mother, father and child under the eyes of a variety of professionals, each with her own expertise. And if physician and medical center are selected with care, the gains outweigh the losses. Do visit the medical center where your doctor practices to find out where to park, where to enter the facility, and what rules and regulations the maternity department asks everyone to observe. If you have a choice of two, choose the one with the best medical staff and equipment over the one which offers free champagne. A hospital with a maternity department should have an anesthesiologist available around the clock. One operating room should be set up at all times for emergency surgery and a laboratory should be available day and night for crucial tests. The staff should be helpful and considerate. And the procedures should not interfere with

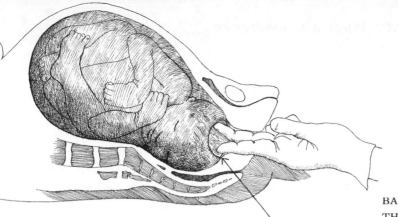

BABY'S HEAD APPEARS THROUGH
THE 5- TO 6-CM DILATED CERVIX

one's privacy and family closeness any more than necessary. There
should be a sound explanation for every rule.

There are two perpetual questions about giving birth in a hospital
which cannot be totally resolved. The first is, At what point should a
woman be admitted? and the second, How can she be protected from the
bacteria carried by someone else?

A woman is generally only admitted to the labor and delivery department when there is no doubt that labor has begun. A physician or midwife
diagnoses labor by reaching with a gloved hand to the back of the vagina
to slide the fingertips over the cervix. During a contraction, a trained
hand can feel the effectiveness of the contractions as well as the progress
of labor and the position of the baby. While you are being examined, don't
concentrate on the nurse's fingers, concentrate on keeping your body relaxed from the waist down. If dilatation is less than 2 cm, the doctor may
suggest that you go home for a while. It may be hours or days before you
need to be in a hospital—but it could also be fairly soon. Keep an eye on
your symptoms and when change in the direction of more active labor
occurs or if there is a sign of a problem, call your doctor again.

In answer to the second question, you will be protected from other people's bacteria partially by the use of sterile technique and because visitors
as well as contacts among patients are usually limited. But the risk of
picking up an infection is still there even if medical personnel, including
doctors, wash their hands before they touch you or your baby. And rules
and regulations can impair spontaneity between parents and infant. Therefore parents often leave the hospital as soon as it is clear that mother
and infant no longer need to have quick access to medical attention.

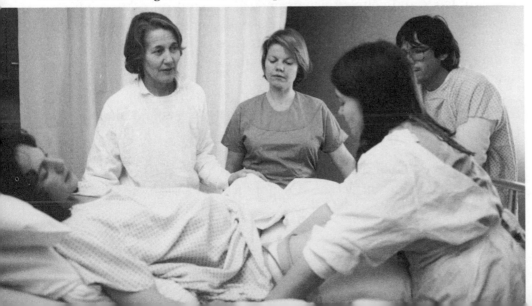

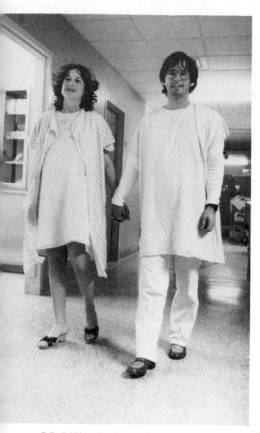

Mobility helps labor progress.

Soon after your arrival, if the examination revealed that you are in labor, make the labor room comfortable with whatever you brought from home: radio or tape recorder, a soft fluffy pillow, warm socks, a favorite chapstick and mouthwash, a pleasant lotion, a lunch and snacks for the coach, paper and pencil to keep a record and other items which comfort you. Do keep these articles to a minimum, for most labor rooms are small and the nurses don't like clutter. Wear loose clothes, comfortable shoes (this especially for the coach) and leave valuables at home. In most hospitals both parties change clothes after admission. The woman in labor puts on a loose comfortable hospital gown which ties in the back and the coach dresses like all other birth attendants—in the outfit surgeons wear before they scrub up for an operation: drawstring pants and a short-sleeved shirt with one wallet-sized pocket. Before entering the delivery room, the coach adds boots over his shoes; a cap to cover his hair and a mask over nose and mouth. The coach might want to eat something high in carbohydrates before going in to prevent sudden queasiness, and he should wash his hands well in preparation for handling the baby.

The professionals and facilities are there for you, the mother in labor, not you for them. Concentrate on handling your labor and let those who can help you. Nurse, coach and doctor can form a perfect support team. Listen to suggestions which help and reject those which do not. If the nurse says, "Open your eyes and focus" and you have discovered that you concentrate better with your eyes closed, tell her. If a nurse or resident is not considerate or makes you nervous, tense or insecure, ask to speak to the person in charge and request that you be served by someone else. If someone says, "You are doing the breathing all wrong," listen and learn what you can, but keep in mind that the perfect technique is the one which works for you.

Your blood pressure and temperature should be checked at regular intervals and so should the baby's heartbeat. But these procedures need not tie you down in bed. Mobility helps labor progress. Don't allow anything to be given to you or done to you without your understanding and approval. All attending members of the medical profession owe you an explanation of procedures you do not immediately understand.

In any labor and delivery department, the sounds of other women in labor are often quite audible. They are usually not sounds of ecstasy. The cries of a person in pain are always distressing to hear, but more so for a woman who is herself in labor. "Is it going to be that bad?" is her first thought.

As a coach, don't ignore such cries in the hope that she did not hear them. Talk about it instead: "Don't let it frighten you, and don't assume that it is someone further along in labor and that you will later lose control too. Maybe she had no preparation or has no one with her. You may well be further dilated than she is. If you need it you can have pain relief. Let's just take one contraction at a time and let's see how far we get."

THE PROGRESS OF LABOR

Once the cervix is 5 cm dilated, neither the mother nor the medical profession will have any doubt as to the diagnosis. Labor is now clearly and perceptibly established and a woman settles down for hard and serious work. How hard and how long remains unpredictable. The first clear sign of progress will be the urge to bear down. Just before that, some women report that they feel the pain change location and move down. Some respond to the last centimeters of dilatation with irritability.

A rupture of membranes once labor is established will result in stronger contractions because the baby's head will press on the cervix and the head is firmer than the water balloon-like amniotic sac. Firm pressure on the cervix triggers a stronger contraction, which brings even firmer pressure on the cervix, resulting in a stronger contraction; thus labor accelerates.

In medieval times, midwives poked at the bulging sac with a sharp nail. Today physicians use a sterile tool to bring this rupture about if it does not occur spontaneously after 5 cm dilatation. The membranes are nerve-free; their rupture feels like a relief until the next and stronger contraction. Then you have to keep in mind that it is by these strong contractions that the process reaches its exciting completion.

At this point getting up to go to the bathroom or climbing on a bedpan may seem a real hassle. There is nothing wrong with wetting the bed; the disposable pad under the buttocks needs to be changed at regular intervals anyway and the area around the vagina should be washed every once in a while too. After the rupture of membranes, each contraction squirts out a little amniotic fluid, and secretions from cervix and vagina are often abundant too.

After the first urge to bear down, a professional birth attendant should check the cervix. If it is fully open, the transition from the dilatation to the expulsion stage went by almost unnoticed. If it is not, you are in for some hard work. Fortunately this transition is usually short. Ask the physician or nurse what the precise findings of the examination were. When the cervix is soft and eight centimeters open, some doctors say "push to comfort," meaning: No all-out bearing down yet, but sneaking in a little push here and there does not matter. This extra pressure during a contraction sometimes completes dilatation sooner. But if the cervix is rigid and somewhat swollen right under the pubic bone (the anterior lip this is called), any extra pressure might make it swell more. In that case you will have to try very hard not to bear down. Sometimes there is less pressure in a side-lying position. Keep in mind that blowing only controls the bearing down pressure which results from holding a breath and compressing the air. It does not control the abdominal muscles. Pushing with those becomes a reflex reaction when the nerves around the rectum receive a certain amount of pressure, and that reflex can be uncontrollable.

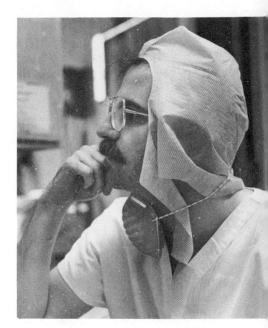

Coach dressed for the delivery room

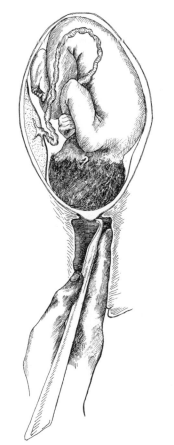

ARTIFICIAL RUPTURE OF MEMBRANES AT APPROXIMATELY 5 CM DILATATION

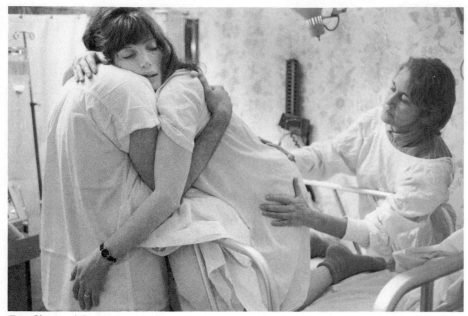
Dealing with back pain

Some women get frightened at this point, with notions that it is too much, that it will never end, that they can do no more. The body may perspire or shake in response to the tumultuous contractions. In some, nausea and throwing up add to the despair. Now the coach comes in. Very carefully and tactfully he acknowledges her pain, then tries to give her perspective: "I know this is hard. It's the hardest part, it won't get any harder. You are doing it now and you are doing so well, maybe one more contraction and you'll be ready to push. Soon we'll have the baby. I can see you are hurting; don't let it frighten you. Let's take one at a time, let's try just one more." In between contractions, coach, don't ask, "Would you like an ice chip, dear?" Offer it to her and if she does not need it she'll push it away. The same holds for other thoughtful gestures. Don't talk about them, do them and if they are not right she'll let you know.

If there was time to reflect in this phase of labor, both of you would wonder what got you into it. Such loss of perspective is quite common during a great strenuous effort. Why you are there will be clear again when you are holding your baby. Just keep your eyes open for signs that the expulsion stage has begun. Those are, first and foremost,

- a distinct increase in the length and/or the intensity of the urges to bear down;
- second, a change in the pattern of the contractions—often they become a little shorter and farther apart again;
- third, a change in the secretions of the vagina—until now there was maybe some pink thick mucus which dislodged from the cervix when dilatation began, then the water from the amniotic sac if it ruptured,

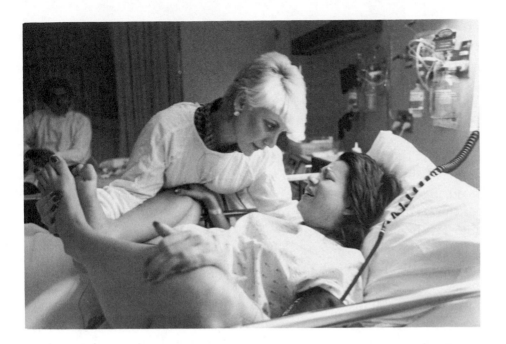

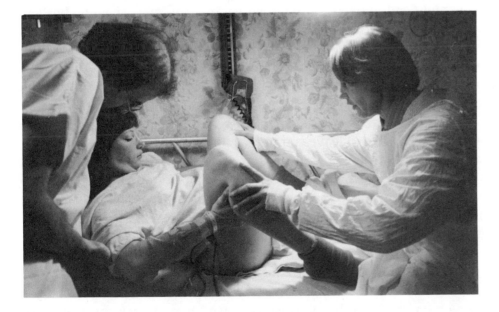

now there may be some bright red blood because the final opening of the cervix sometimes tears some small blood vessels;

- finally, a change in the mother's mood—sometimes a woman having a difficult time may become almost impossible. "No more," she will say, "I don't want to do this anymore." Sometimes the mood improves instead. In short, during transition look for change and when it occurs ask the doctor, midwife or nurse to check if the expulsion stage has begun.

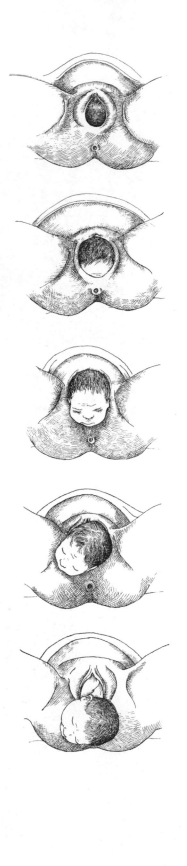

If it has, a whole new set of responses is called for. And it may well take a few contractions before the pushing goes smoothly. Encouragement and—where necessary—suggestions and corrections are usually a great help. Many women say they can feel the baby move down, but that will not be the only sensation. Pressure and stretching are part of it too. And there is often still pain, different perhaps from that of dilatation, but still it hurts.

Remember that the birth passage curves toward the back then forward. When the baby is in this bend to the back, there may be a few contractions during which it appears to the mother that birth just might happen out of the rectum. Then the baby pivots up around the pubic bone to the vagina. The baby appears at this opening when the mother pushes with a contraction and it slips out of sight when she stops. It may take a few contractions before the baby remains visible. Then the skin around the vagina starts to stretch. The mother may feel a burning or tingling sensation which often numbs when the baby comes down a little farther, where the pressure from its head temporarily closes the blood vessels, often lessening the perception of pain. Now the doctor or midwife gently massages the area under pressure while guiding the head. When the full circumference of the head appears in the open vagina, the mother stops bearing down. She blows with relaxed lips and concentrates on keeping the muscles around her vagina and those which control movement of the legs fully relaxed—the head is born better with the pushing force from the uterus alone; such a controlled birth is easier on the baby's head and on the mother's birth passage.

The mixture of great pain, true relief, ecstasy and other sensations on feeling her baby's head leave is different for each woman each time. The shoulders usually emerge more easily. The mother feels the pressure mount when they line up to exit. An easy push from her with gentle pressure downward on the head from the birth attendant releases the upper shoulder from behind the pubic bone, then when the head is lifted up a little, the lower shoulder slips out. And within a few moments, the mother will feel a wet slippery sensation, and the baby is born.

In the delivery room it is customary to have a large mirror placed so the mother and her coach can see the birth. Your first glance at the baby's head as it emerges will be awe-inspiring, whether you are the mother or father. Remind yourselves that the bulging of the area around the vagina will not last past the birth. Also that the baby does not have an unusually small head, but that only part of it is visible, the remainder is what causes the bulging. The baby's skin may appear loose; this happens when the bones of its head temporarily overlap to fit the birth passage. The hair will be wet and may have specks of white or red. The white is vernix caseosa, the cheesy stuff with which some newborns are covered, and the red is blood. The last centimeters of dilatation can tear a small vessel in the cervix and, in passing through, the baby may pick up a drop of the

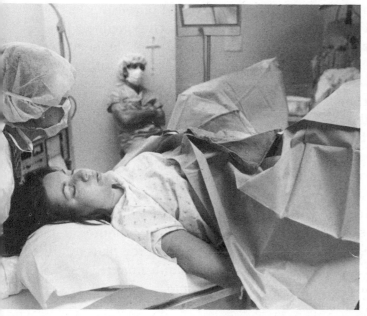

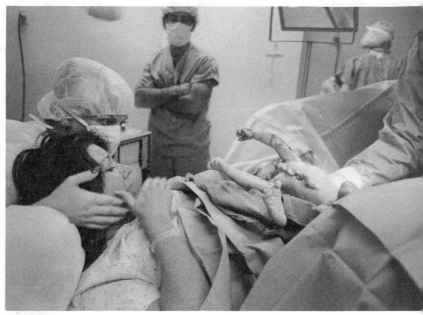

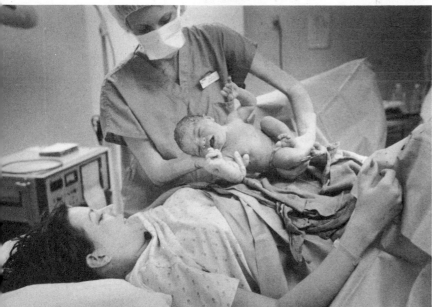

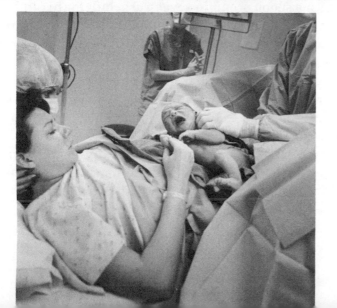

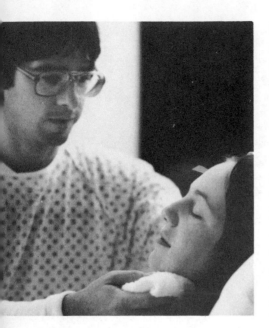

blood. The skin color may range from reddish pink to purple at plus-five station. It will change to pink once the baby is born. The shoulders don't quite look like shoulders until they are out. The birth of the shoulders often releases a gush of amniotic fluid, which may be pink rather than clear if there are a few drops of blood mixed in with it. If you can, watch your baby unfold and change those first moments after birth.

The detachment of the placenta may well remain unnoticed until doctor or midwife says, "Give me one more push." It slips out much more easily than the baby. Now the pregnancy hormones stop flowing. This allows the release of the ones which will fill the breasts with milk. This sudden hormonal change, combined with the tremendous energy just exerted, often gives a new mother the shakes. A warm blanket will feel nice and the trembling will stop soon—usually within five to twenty minutes. Some doctors like to examine the placental site to make sure the placenta detached completely. This examination lasts less than a minute. Use the panting technique of breathing if it is uncomfortable.

GUIDELINES FOR THE COACH

Now let's look again at the process of delivery, this time with specific guidelines for the coach.

Women react very differently to labor. Some perspire, and like to have a wet washcloth to wipe with. Some become cold (especially the feet); for them a hot-water bottle or wool socks are quite nice. Some who practiced primarily because they loved all the touching cannot bear to be touched during labor. Others will not let their coach take his hands away. Others enjoy a good backrub in between contractions. A few use these short breaks to doze off. Thus a coach needs to be open-minded, not planning to do this, that and the next thing, but watching alertly to see what helps her, even if this is sitting silently next to the bed.

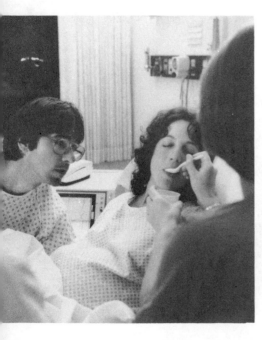

If her lips appear dry, moisten them at regular intervals with a chapstick. The lining of the mouth may need moistening too. A few pieces of crushed ice given with a spoon or put in a wet washcloth for her to suck on will moisten the mouth and throat without much water reaching the stomach. During active labor nausea can result or increase if she drinks, and the acidic digestive juices would start to flow. And a general anesthetic is more safely administered when the stomach content is neutral. Thus the anesthesiologist's advice to pregnant women has become: "Don't eat when you think you're in labor—not even candy—because it increases the possibility of complications should it be necessary to put you out for a few moments." Many labor and delivery departments observe a "nothing by mouth" rule. In that case let her rinse her mouth at regular intervals with plain water, not mouthwash, which tends to make the lining of the mouth more dry.

Relaxation between contractions can be quite difficult for the mother, especially if she is not aware she is holding shoulder or hip muscles tense. If stroking or kneading these areas does not relax them ask her to tighten as tight as she can her arms, legs, buttocks, shoulders, then to relax. Repeat this a few times to help remind her of the difference between tension and relaxation.

When you help her with the breathing remember that she should:

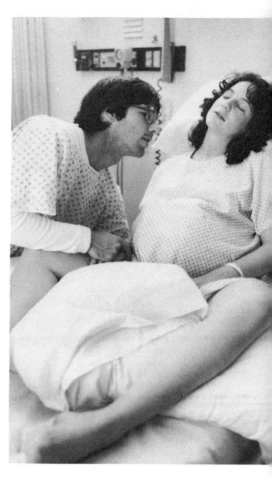

- breathe slowly and deeply when possible, and switch to a more superficial, more rapid breathing only when a contraction dictates, then return to slower and deeper breathing when that contraction eases;
- breathe in and out rhythmically and easily. For each breath in there is an equal one out. The in is silent, the out is barely audible;
- not hold her breath during dilatation contractions;
- try to start and always finish a contraction with a cleansing breath.

Hyperventilation is more likely to occur when she uses the panting for the major part of a contraction. Help her breathe in as much as out. If she complains about a prickly feeling around her mouth or a tingling in the fingers help her overcome her body's upset chemical balance (a lack of carbon dioxide in her system) by asking her to hold her breath and tighten her arms for 5 to 10 seconds a few times in between contractions. Breath holding and muscle tension will help the body regain the carbon dioxide balance. If she continues to hyperventilate discuss the problem with the doctor or nurse. You can sometimes remedy hyperventilation by blowing up a paper sandwich bag, then giving it to her and letting her breathe in and out of the bag for some of each contraction. Make sure she takes a few cleansing breaths when the contraction is over.

Don't panic if she loses control during a contraction every once in a while. Once a woman cries out in pain and tenses her body it is almost impossible to help her gain control during that contraction. Help her to accept that she just lost one and encourage her to try again with the next one. Maybe the next one won't be quite so hard or so long. Be sincere. Never make light of her pain. And if she says it is too much, discuss with your birth attendants what kind of pain relief is most appropriate for the situation.

At the onset of the bearing down reflex remember that she should try to control the urge to bear down by blowing until the birth attendant has diagnosed a fully open cervix.

During expulsion help her:
- position the body correctly then work, but not overwork.
- aim for correct muscle use rather than strenuous pushing. This means she compresses air in the chest, not in the face, and tries to hold it for at least 5 seconds and not more than 10. During a quick forced exhalation she maintains the pressure from the contracted abdominal muscles, but the muscles surrounding the birth passage are relaxed at all times.
- bear down for the full length of a contraction and rest in between.

No matter how well you practiced, it will most likely take a few real expulsive contractions to put these skills into practice during labor. You cannot learn skiing except on a slope. Preliminary instructions only speed up your mastery of the sport. It is the same with labor. A patient and articulate coach can be a great help. Briefly review how she is to push after complete dilatation has been diagnosed, but before the first pushing contraction begins: "When you feel a contraction start, let it build up by taking a cleansing breath. Then take in a medium-sized breath, hold it, block it in your chest, lean on it, and push. Bring your chin toward your chest and your shoulders forward and downward. Bend your elbows up and forward and pull with your hands on your legs (or on the handlebars on the side of the delivery table). When you are ready, breathe out forcefully and in quickly, then take in a quick gulp of air. Keep the abdominal pressure on the baby while you exchange air. Keep the hip muscles relaxed." After this many words, a contraction is likely to start. When that one is over make the necessary corrections.

Don't forget to take care of yourself while you help her. Sit on the edge of the bed or pull up a chair whenever possible. Bring something to eat to the hospital and include a favorite carbohydrate snack. If eating that just before entering the delivery room does not prevent queasiness and you feel yourself becoming dizzy, don't be embarrassed; you've probably worked hard for many hours. Pull your mask down so you can breathe better. If that does not help, sit down with your head between your knees. If the dizziness continues, lie down before you fall down, because the floor in the delivery room is hard. Of the hundreds of men I have taught, as far as I know only two passed out, both after the baby was born when the tension was gone and it was clear that everything was fine.

All through her labor be open to the suggestions of those around you and let the nurses help you where they can. Being a good coach does not depend on being the only coach.

Further instructions or more predictions are not realistic. The average length of labor or duration of contractions among American women is only a statistic to guide professionals, not a number to cling to as you prepare for birth. For both of you, birth remains a life process: variable, changeable, subtle. It cannot be captured. It has to be lived, and each person's life is that person's task. Information, advice and support can help, but the remainder is up to you.

Part Four

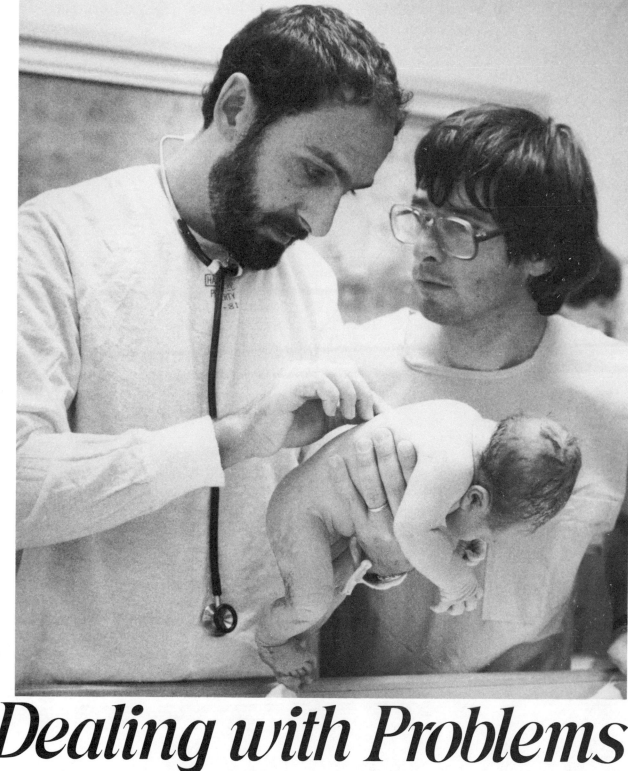

Dealing with Problems
& Complications

HANDLING FEAR

The ancient and tenacious fear of birth is becoming less and less justified, not because fewer problems occur, but because medicine has found a remedy for most. There was a time when a pregnant woman would ease her anxieties by slipping a smooth stone inside her dress and as it fell to the ground wishing that her baby would leave her just as easily when the time came. Today she can tell herself, "If nature runs into a problem, the doctor will be able to help."

The stone method is called sympathetic magic. All of us, including scientists, need a little of it when we find ourselves confronted with our human limitations. During those nights when the dread of labor keeps sleep away, try to find some belief or activity behind which you can organize your fears. If you choose something as rational as exercising or practicing the skills for birth, realize that while such practicing may increase your ability to deal with what labor has in store, it will not affect labor itself because it does not change one's genetic structure. It will be a help, not a guarantee. Therefore if one of your classmates reports a long labor, don't get discouraged. Without her skills and endurance, her labor would have been harder to handle. And keep in mind that neither long nor short labors are contagious. But fear is.

Of all the emotions I have watched in myself and in others, fear has puzzled me the most. When it becomes an incentive for action I think of it as a creative emotion. But when it blinds or paralyzes, I wonder why evolution has allowed such a response. Of all my emotions, I fear my own fear the most. I find the anticipation of suffering is worse than the suffering itself. When pain is actually there, reality changes and we cope, but when we are sitting comfortably, sipping tea with a friend who tells of her horrible labor, fear can just leap out of bounds.

Many people do not talk with a pregnant woman about pain and danger in labor. They believe that her anticipation can bring on more suffering than she otherwise would have. But every woman knows of friends whose labor was hard or who needed medical assistance. So I think such forced silence does not help. And it can leave a woman unprepared when knowledge might be of crucial importance. Therefore I believe it is better to be aware of potential problems and to know the signs of complications.

Accept your own and your partner's fears and let them become part of the fuel which spurs you on to good performance. Think about, talk about and practice the skills until they become yours. Select a physician or midwife with care, then discuss with this person, who now shares in the responsibility for your well-being, your hopes and your fears. And keep the stone method in mind. Think about what you wish most for this birth. Wishing, like praying, is personal and private, and a little sympathetic magic can't hurt.

THE USE OF PAIN RELIEF

Western medicine has always set itself two goals—to prolong life and ease pain. The ability to relieve labor pain is new and has only in the last twenty years been perfected to the point where it no longer needs to mean an altered consciousness, being put out, or a drugged baby. Medical practitioners are proud of this achievement, justifiably I think, and why a woman would turn it down without due consideration is beyond the comprehension of many physicians.

The rule that it is best to keep pain relievers to a minimum is a good one, but drugs do have their uses. Sometimes a small dose of the right pain relief is beneficial, either for the progress of labor or for the mother. Therefore ask your physician what type of pain relief will be available to you and what the effects might be on you or your baby. If this discussion reinforces your desire to avoid medications, tell him or her not that you insist you won't use a pain killer, but that you would like to try not to. Explain that you understand it may be difficult and that this is why you are bringing it up. Tell your doctor that when labor gets difficult you will be counting on his support. Will he/she be able to give you encouragement and perspective? When in spite of encouragement from coach and nurse a woman begins to give into the feeling that it is too much, her doctor can often restore some of her confidence in herself and trust in the process again.

SIGNS OF A COMPLICATION

Since it is customary today that a woman spends early labor at home by herself or with her partner, both should be aware not only of the normal symptoms of labor, but also of signs of trouble. This will enable you to call right at the onset of a problem should one occur, and it also facilitates coaching. At four in the morning when the doctor says, "Call me back at six," a woman can lose her perspective and begin to fear that it hurts more than it should, therefore something is wrong. To say, "No, there is nothing wrong, everything is normal, let's just deal with your contractions one at a time until six," will be easier when you know the symptoms of complications.

Coach, you should keep an eye on the expectant mother's general appearance. An overall puffiness with dizziness, a headache and blurred vision or dots floating in front of her eyes can be signs of a blood pressure problem.

Check her temperature at hourly intervals. A rise in temperature of .5° or more can be the mark of the beginning of an infection or of too great a fluid loss.

Be aware of the type and location of the pain she is experiencing. Constant severe pain in an abdomen which remains firm is a sign of trouble. The pain of labor when it is felt in the abdomen should wax and wane; it does not always completely subside but it should ease when a contraction is over. Constant abdominal pain and firmness can be a sign that the placenta has begun to detach. But constant and even severe pain in the lower back is not a danger sign, just something very hard to cope with.

Both of you should be aware of the amount of bleeding from the vagina. There is a distinct difference between a bloody discharge, which is not common but normal, and bleeding. The first is a mixture of mucus and blood which comes free when a small vessel in the cervix breaks. The latter is blood which flows freely to soak a napkin in half an hour or less. Such bleeding usually means that the placenta lies over the cervix and has started to detach with dilatation.

If the membranes rupture check the color of the fluid which escapes. It should be clear. Small specks of white in this watery fluid are particles of the vernix caseosa and are normal. A green color is caused by the baby's release of meconium, a waste-like product from the bowels. Such release before birth can mean that the baby is under stress.

If you notice one of these signs of trouble call physician or midwife without delay. If the doctor can't be reached immediately, the woman in labor should lie on her left side, continue to breathe easily, and try to release tension wherever it pops up. That way the mind is focused on what needs to be done rather than becoming obsessed with the problem.

The basic skills behind birth preparation have been with us for centuries. While breathing techniques have only recently been adapted to labor, the concept behind them, that of using the breath to center oneself, is an ancient one conceived by mystics who taught themselves centering in order to live through change, stress and pain.

THE BABY DURING LABOR

The baby's well-being during labor is assessed by its heartbeat. A fetal monitor is thought to give the most accurate reading and is therefore always used when the doctor anticipates a problem, and quite often before then. This monitor prints two graphs, one of the baby's heartbeat and one of the contractions. It allows the coach to see the exact moment a contraction starts, peaks, subsides and ends. Mother and coach can also watch their baby's response to labor. Uterine contractions have the potential of interfering with the baby's circulation and such interference will alter its heartbeat. Physicians have learned how to tell a placenta which cannot handle contractions from a loop or knot in the cord by reading the graph. Sometimes a change in the mother's position corrects the heart-

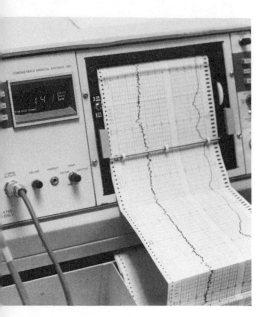

beat by improving the circulation. If not, further examination of the baby may be necessary. The heart of a well baby beats irregularly; the graph is an ever-changing line. Whenever this line becomes straight, with dips during a contraction which only slowly return to what it was before, the baby is asking for immediate help.

CORD PROLAPSE

If, after the rupture of membranes, the cord should become visible at the vagina, kneel on all fours and rest your chin on your hands (the knee-chest position). With the buttocks thus elevated, the baby will press less on its own cord. Should this happen at home, the coach should wash his hands well and slip the fingers of one hand along the cord up into the vagina to where they touch the baby, then press the baby gently upward, away from the cord, to keep it from compressing its lifeline. An ambulance will take the mother to the medical center in this position. There the physicians will know how to help the baby out of its precarious situation.

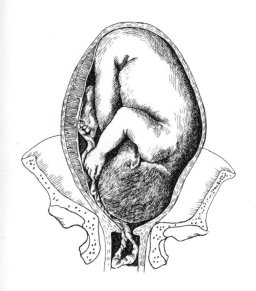

Knee-chest position

FOOT PROLAPSE

Occasionally when a baby has chosen the buttocks-down position, rupture of the membranes can allow one foot to slip out with the water. Don't push it back in; if it happens at home call the doctor and be off to the medical center, preferably in the knee-chest position (to prevent prolapse of the cord), knowing that your baby's one foot looks awfully cute. Once there, you and your doctor will decide what the best road to life for your baby is: through the vagina or through the abdomen.

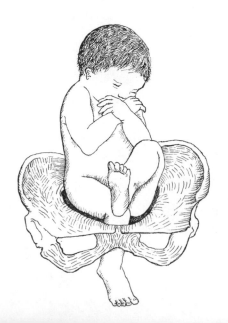

ABOUT A CESAREAN SECTION

Midwives and mothers dreamed of the ability to create an emergency exit through the abdomen without endangering mother or baby for centuries before it became a reality. The cesarean section has displaced some pretty archaic techniques, such as letting nature take its course or using forceps to pull a baby through a tight passage. I agree that surgery is sometimes used unnecessarily. However, when complications set in, or when hours of strong contractions produce no dilatation, one cannot help but be grateful that physicians today know how to help mother and baby out by this simple operation.

Of all the surgery I have seen—I was an operating room nurse for seven years—this one is the most inspiring to watch. If possible, the mother is awake and she is given a spinal or an epidural anesthesia to block out perception of sensations below the waist. She will have a general anesthetic only when the problem demands it.

I don't believe anyone can face surgery without fear. Therefore allow it to be there, then use the technique of concentrating on breathing, of releasing tension each time it creeps up, and of dealing with what needs to be done to keep your mind from running away and possibly fighting your body.

As a coach, if you are able to stay during the surgery, continue to use the same supportive techniques. Be honest. Don't discount her fear or her pain, but accept those feelings and help her deal with them. You will be afraid too, but when both of you share and accept your feelings, a lasting bond of strength and support will be spun between you.

The position for administering a spinal or epidural block is side-lying with the knees and the chin pulled toward the chest to align the vertebrae and increase the space between them. While the anesthesiologist concentrates on the fine skill of placing the local anesthetic close to the nerves which supply the body from the waist down with sensations, the nurse holds the mother so she will not move inadvertently. Contractions can be difficult to handle in this position. One, maybe two, will pass before the anesthetic takes effect. *As her coach,* talk to her with the same relaxed voice you used before. Place your hands where it helps her as long as you don't get into the anesthesiologist's way.

Once the local anesthetic has taken effect, the mother is helped to return to the supine position. A folded sheet may be placed under her right hip to keep the uterus off the vena cava, allowing for better circulation in mother and baby. The nurse will slip a catheter in the bladder to keep it empty and out of the way. After the nurse shaves and washes her abdomen, the obstetrician and one other physician will cover the mother with sterile sheets. One of these sheets is pinned up to form a screen between

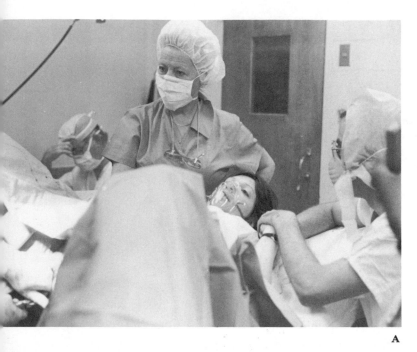

A

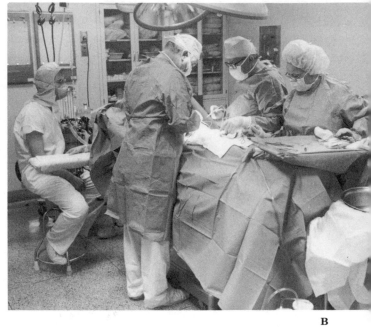

B

After an unsuccessful attempt with forceps (A), the mother is quickly prepared for a cesarean section (B). The father photographs his baby as it emerges (C), then takes the newborn to meet his mother (D).

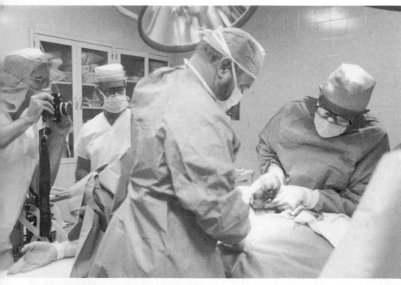

C

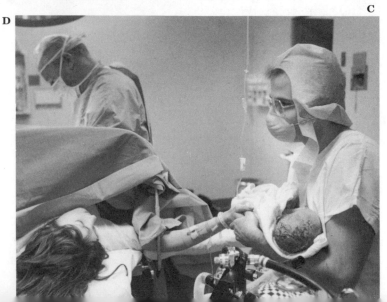

D

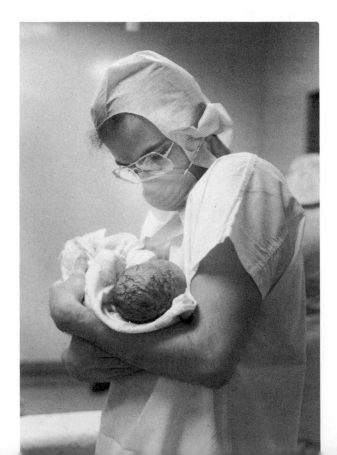

the sterile field of the surgeon and the area where the anesthesiologist works. Now woman and coach are protected from seeing the actual operation. Within minutes the highly skillful team opens the skin, separates the muscles and opens the uterus. Then the baby is lifted out, suctioned, and after the cord is severed it is handed to the pediatrician for care and evaluation. While the placenta is removed, the uterus closed, the muscles moved back together and stitches placed in the skin, the new parents can enjoy their infant. If the mother's hands were tied at the start of the operation, she can ask now to have them freed so she can touch and play with her baby. The head of a baby born through the abdomen is usually not molded by the birth canal. This gives the newborn that "beautifully formed" look characteristic of a surgically delivered baby.

If a general anesthetic is used, the preparatory procedures of placing the catheter, shaving the abdomen and sometimes even the placing of sterile sheets are done before it is administered. This way the baby will be delivered before the anesthetic crosses the placenta.

THE USE OF FORCEPS

If the baby needs to be turned because it did not turn its head correctly in labor, or if it needs to be helped past a narrowing in the birth passage, forceps or traction by suction may be used. While surgery has replaced the older technique of pulling a baby all the way through a tight pelvis, brief traction on a baby who only needs help to get past a tight spot is considered better than an operation. Sometimes a doctor puts the forceps on to discover that it will require too much pull. Then the mother is quickly prepared for an abdominal delivery. Sometimes the mother is asked to bear down while the coach counts, the obstetrician pulls and the anesthesiologist presses on the top of the uterus. Such team work seems to come naturally to human beings. The desire to help others is a very human trait. Therefore, after a forceps delivery don't say, "I could not do it naturally." Say, "I could not do it all by myself." One wonders what such a birth is like from the baby's point of view. Hold it and talk to it, if possible. Whenever birth is more difficult, parents and baby need to reassure each other that all is well.

It is customary to give the mother spinal or epidural anesthesia during a forceps delivery. But as with an abdominal birth, there are occasional medical problems which indicate the use of general anesthesia. During the administration of a general anesthetic, you can still hear even after you can no longer tell others you hear them, and on waking up, you hear again before you feel like responding. Thus to help a person who is being induced into this deep sleep, talk with a very gentle and caring voice: "Breathe in and out; you are doing so well; just let yourself go to sleep now. When you wake up the baby will be here." And when she begins to wake up: "You are waking up now. The baby is fine. You are fine too. This is your baby. Your baby is fine." During this gentle small talk centered on her, show her the baby, if possible. By your talk you help her bridge the gap created by her anesthetic.

Sometimes the coach is asked to leave. Some doctors have little confidence in the father's ability to remain centered and supportive to a loved one undergoing surgery, and some lack trust in themselves. Some coaches would rather not be there. In such a case, encourage her to use the techniques as if she hears you and remind her that you'll be with her as soon as you can.

Occasionally after all has gone well with the birth, the placenta refuses to detach or its detachment causes severe bleeding. Now the doctor needs to examine the inside of the uterus. If no pain relief was used for the birth, a general anesthetic may be quickest and therefore the method of choice.

EMERGENCY CHILDBIRTH

While some babies journey through the birth passage slowly, others make the trip unusually fast. They surprise their parents along the freeway or in their own bedroom. A birth this easy rarely poses a problem as long as you observe some very basic rules:

If the baby comes, let it come. Don't hold it back by closing the legs. It will come out with some force and be wet and slippery. Don't rely on your ability to catch it. Place your body so that the baby cannot fall: lie on the floor, on a bed, or sideways on the car seat. Blow during a contraction, let just the uterus cause the birth. Accept the pressure, let the body stretch open. Keep the buttocks relaxed, open the knees and bring them toward the trunk, relax the hip muscles. The head is the largest part. Allow it to slip out; the shoulders will come easier and the baby will then slide out.

The color of a baby at birth is not as important as its color five minutes later. What you look for in assessing the well-being of a newborn is the rate with which it progresses toward becoming a pink, kicking, responsive baby. At the side of the road or on the floor in the living room, lift the baby out of the puddle of water with one hand under its head, neck and shoulders and the other hand under and around its buttocks. Place it on the mother's abdomen. Dry it off. Then cover it to keep it from cooling. Leave the cord intact even when the placenta slips out.

Some bleeding after the placenta comes out is normal. If there is a steady flow of blood, stimulate the nipples and massage the uterus to help it contract. Just knead the lower abdomen but don't push down on it toward the vagina. And get to a hospital as soon as possible if the bleeding does not decrease significantly.

The only time you would cut the cord when birth takes place without professional help is when the baby is entangled in it. After the head has emerged, if the cord is around the neck it will be visible as a silvery shiny necklace. Take this necklace with the fingers of both hands. Pull on it gently to see if a loop large enough to slip over the head can be made. If so, the baby is free. If not, the cord is holding it back from being born. Sever it with whatever is available, if necessary the teeth. The cord has no nerves, so severing it does not hurt either mother or child. Once the baby is born, its side of the cord should be clamped or tied as soon as possible otherwise the baby will lose blood. Do this at the very end of the cord away from the baby. When help arrives, someone with sterile equipment can cut it closer to the navel.

If you can see that the baby is about to arrive buttocks or feet first (a breech birth), get into the knee-chest position (see page 144) and blow—to keep from pushing—until professional help arrives. In the breech position a baby often needs help with the birth of its head. If the baby is going to come no matter what, turn over onto your back if you can, and let its body slip out. If the head does not follow, give a good push and if necessary another one. Refrain from lifting the baby and pulling; this will interfere with its alignment inside and make the birth of the head more rather than less difficult. Remember that nature has done this before, but you have not. Only an obstetrician has through careful observation, study and practice acquired the ability to change the position of a baby still in the birth canal without hurting it or hampering the process.

INFANT RESUSCITATION

Occasionally a baby does not breathe right after birth. Its air passage may be obstructed by mucus. The problems which can arise from not breathing are immediately magnified when the baby cools off. So even when a baby comes out purple or white and unresponsive, lift it quickly out of the puddle of water which escaped with the birth of the shoulders, dry it off as you place it loosely covered with a sweater or jacket on the mother's abdomen. Place the baby on its side. If you can do so without losing time, place a folded handkerchief or a bunch of Kleenex under its shoulder because this slight stretch at the neck will prevent its tongue from obstructing the air passage. Now lean forward and gently suck with your mouth or with a suction bulb first its nose and then its mouth, to clear them of obstruction. Stimulate the baby by rubbing gently along its spine with your fingertips. Watch carefully for movement and for improvement in color. If this does not occur, give the baby mouth-to-mouth breathing. Place your mouth over the baby's nose and mouth. Make the breaths small; a baby has tiny lungs: one count in, pause for a count out, one count in again, and give just little puffs of air. Continue until more skilled help and equipment are available.

To learn more complete resuscitation techniques—important skills not

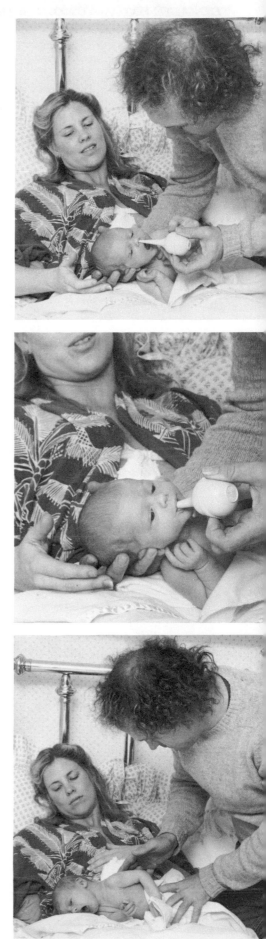

only for the birth but for the raising of children—take a Red Cross class in resuscitation, or one taught by the American Heart Association.

HANDLING GRIEF

It happens rarely now, but still an infant occasionally does not survive. Birth and death, though at opposite ends of our lives, are not always a long distance apart. When an infant dies before, or shortly after birth, there may be great sorrow. And like pain, sorrow will increase if you fight it. So allow yourself to grieve. If you let yourself experience fully whatever sadness life brings, your pain will lift much sooner and more completely than it will for people who fight the need to grieve.

But don't linger on in darkness any longer than necessary. Don't pause to say "I should have" or "Why me?" Those are irrelevant questions. You did what you could. Just keep on going, slowly and carefully at first, toward a lighter place. Father and mother need to support each other and protect each other from people who may be unintentionally thoughtless. Sorrow is a private affair, and each of us settles it at our own center. And by doing so, we emerge stronger and deeper. We are all creative, and can use such a loss as a turning point toward greater strength and understanding.

Fear may take over again. Don't repress it; use it instead to build courage and caution, essential ingredients for a good life.

Part Five

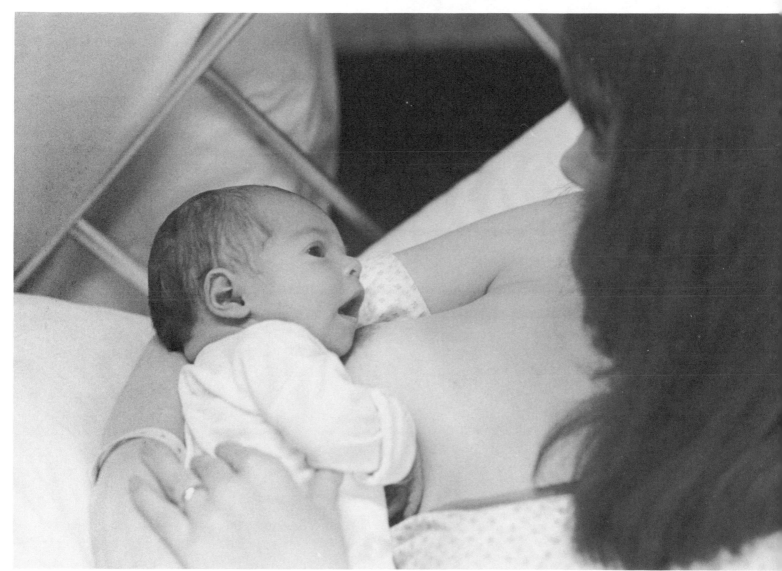

Receiving Your Infant & Nursing

THE BABY AT BIRTH

Second only to the phenomenal event of conception, birth is the greatest transformation of human life. When the newborn's lungs take oxygen out of the air and give off carbon dioxide, the blood changes routes. Instead of receiving just enough blood for their own growth and maintenance, its lungs now receive all the blood for this vital exchange. The flow to and from the placenta ceases. When the sediment-rich river which came in at the navel stops flowing, the liver looks toward the bowels for food. The digestive system awakens, and the infant receives from its mother's breasts a fluid which coats its delicate stomach and raises the infant's ability to defend itself against infection. Next to breathing and to protection from infection, an infant at birth has one more physical need: to be kept warm. Loss of body warmth is a serious threat to its delicate metabolism. If on leaving the soft lining and stable warmth of the mother's body, the skin registers a temperature drop, the baby may cry vigorously. Inside the uterus the infant practiced breathing, sucking, swallowing, urinating and discharging waste through the bowels. At birth it adds a new skill: that of calling its parents' attention to its needs. And being human, its needs are more than just physical. The physical needs are fundamental, but when they are taken care of, needs of a different nature arise that are more difficult to label and appear to vary from infant to infant. Some like to be held, talked to and touched. Others emerge looking for the breast. Some protest vigorously when put in a warm bath. Others stretch and yawn on touching the water as if to say, "Just what I had in mind."

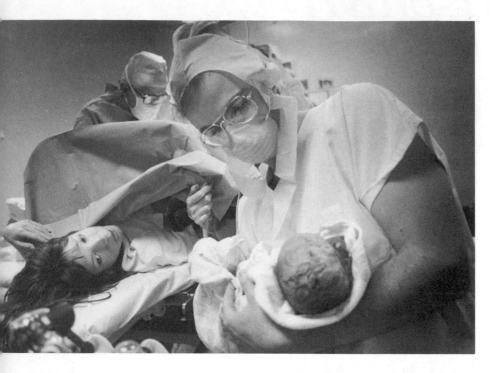

New parents used to exclaim, "Ah, she has my sister's eyebrows and your father's nose. Isn't she cute? Look at her fingers and those tiny nails!" And then they'd kiss her or cry or just stare or they'd hug each other. Today, many solemnly announce, "We took Lamaze," or "We went all the way natural," and "His Apgar is good; we want to do Le Boyer and bond for a while."

After the mechanization of childbirth it became weighted down with psychological jargon. Neither belongs there. Birth is a private event and the initial stage of parenthood is among life's more tender moments. Leave methods and labels behind and trust your responses. Let your innermost feelings help you meet the needs of your child. Each person's responses are truly his own.

Usually the safeguarding of mother and baby does not interfere with their meeting each other. If it does, keep priorities in mind. If an obstructed air passage needs to be cleared, oxygen comes before cuddling or nursing. If a major complication delays the initial meeting, the only harm that is done is that some lovely moments are missed. Here as always human nature is flexible and capable of compensation.

The gaze of a newborn intensifies when someone talks to it, and its eyes seem to search for the origin of the voice. When it finds the speaker's face its focus is not constant. Its eyes look, turn away, then return again (like adults, infants need privacy). Though the amount of holding babies need may vary, all newborns like to be held; but none like the feeling that they might fall and most cannot hold up their heads. When holding your baby, avoid sudden movements and support the head in alignment with the back. Let your baby lean rather than slump.

A FIRST TRY AT NURSING

Some newborns actively look for the breast. Their heads will turn toward the person holding them while the lips open and close in a searching fashion. Even babies who do not show this rooting behavior usually enjoy contact with the breast. If medical conditions permit, mother and baby should be ready for a first playful try at nursing within an hour after birth.

Nursing while flat on one's back is always difficult but more so when it is the first time. Therefore wait until it is possible to turn on your side or to sit up. If you have not washed your hands since the birth, do so now before touching the nipple or the baby's mouth. Place your baby so that its body falls against yours; "tummy to tummy" is the breast-feeding expert's phrase. In a sitting position, well supported by pillows, hold the baby in your right arm if you are left-handed so your left hand is free to manipulate the nipple. When your baby's head rests in the bend of your right elbow, the right hand will fit on its butt or thigh. The baby's left arm and shoulder should be turned down so they will not be compressed when you pull her close. Expose your right breast. Place the index finger above and the other three fingers below the nipple, close to where the skin gets darker. Lift the baby to the breast and touch its lips with the nipple. If after a few touches and strokes the baby does not open its mouth, there is no interest in nursing yet. Try again later. If the baby opens its mouth, pull it closer and slip the nipple well into its mouth. If the baby sucks, the nipple will be pulled between its tongue and palate and its sucking movements will allow the gums to rub and slightly press on the dark skin or areola while the tongue and palate grasp and release, grasp and release the nipple, resulting in what we call suckling. If the baby takes only the nipple and is sucking just on that, break the suction by slipping a clean finger from the corner of its mouth between the gums. Then take the nipple out and start over. The baby may well get furious and you nervous. That's okay. You are both learning a new skill and in the process you are getting to know each other. Keep trying until: (1) the nipple and a bit of the dark part behind the nipple are in the baby's mouth, (2) you can feel the sensation caused by suckling inside your breast, (3) the baby does not just smack its lips but the muscles of its cheeks near the jaws are working too, and (4) the baby swallows off and on. Now lean back and release any unnecessary tension in your arms and shoulders. Maybe your partner can slide a pillow or two under the arm holding the baby. These pillows are especially helpful after an abdominal delivery. Look at your baby: its head should be supported in alignment with its body, and its neck should not be turned to reach the breast. Instead, the baby faces the breast and its body cuddles against yours.

Every baby has its own eating pattern from the very start. But these patterns have a few things in common. First, no matter how hungry it is, a baby will take rest breaks from suckling. During such a break, its lips and

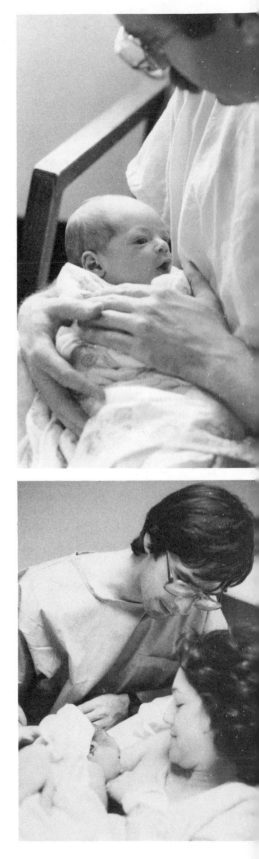

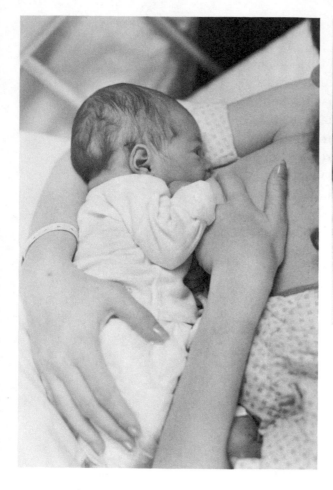

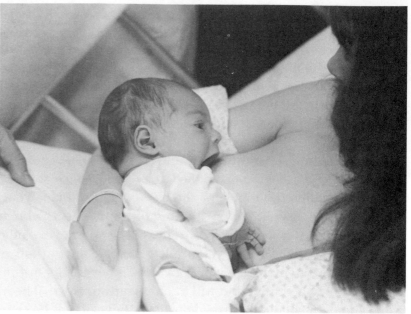

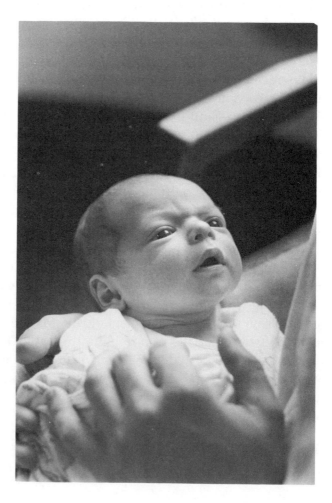

jaws need to rest, but it does not want to lose the nipple. If it slips out even a little, the baby gets tense and restless. If the I-am-losing-the-nipple feeling continues, the baby arches its back and cries. Make sure baby and breast are supported in such a manner that this tension over a rest break does not develop. Do not prod a baby to resume suckling. It will when it is ready. Babies also swallow air while nursing. Almost all babies do it and this air in the stomach bothers them. Some may squirm or show other signs of restlessness while still at the breast, others are only bothered by it later. When the baby squirms, or after five to ten minutes of good feeding when there is a lull in the suction, take the nipple out of its mouth. The baby will probably try to hang on. If so, break the suction before taking the nipple out. Breaking the suction can be done by pulling gently on a corner of the baby's mouth or by slipping a clean finger in between the gums. Hold the baby up to help it bring up the air. Then, if necessary, change a wet or soiled diaper before offering the other breast. If the baby does not do a lot of swallowing while nursing on the second breast, it is no longer eating but merely enjoying the breast. It may not be necessary to burp it again. Mother and baby can both relax and maybe nap in their newfound closeness.

Some say the duration of the first contact with the breast should be limited. Some prescribe the exact length of time: after three, five, nay six minutes exactly, they say, break the suction and take the baby off the breast to prevent nipple soreness. But no two women's breasts are exactly alike, and no two infants have the same needs. How then do I prevent problems? you may wonder. How does the milk come in? Will it be good enough? How do I keep my nipples from getting sore?

Beneath these anxious questions lies a bigger one about motherhood. How do I help a life more precious than my own attain independence? By your very best efforts and by the ability to observe, learn, and act on your knowledge.

HELPING YOUR BREASTS PRODUCE MILK

The ability to make milk depends on the presence of tiny glands in the breasts, not on breast size. Very small breasts often produce in abundance. Production is encouraged every time the baby takes the nipple and suckles, thus sending the message to the mother's brain that milk needs to be produced. Frequent contact between baby and breast also prevents accumulation of this newly secreted fluid, thus lessening the initial swelling response of the breasts. Fortunately motherhood starts with a few days during which a woman enjoys nothing more than admiring her baby and watching it closely to look after its needs, including its frequent desire to suckle. And the intricate web between mother and baby is spun—the

mother needs her baby physically to take her milk; emotionally to love; and intellectually, with her new sense of responsibility. And the baby loves its mother before it loves itself.

During those first days while the mother concentrates totally on the baby's demands, others will take care of her. The ensuing rest combined with the total focus on the infant help body and mind make the adjustment to motherhood. To help your body perform: rest when the baby is calm, drink frequently, not just milk but water and fruit juice, and continue the habit of nibbling on nutritious light snacks. A somewhat bland but well-balanced diet of fresh foods which generally agree with you is best at the start. Avoid those foods which tend to disagree with you. Foods which you do not digest well are more likely to cause your baby problems too. Well balanced means in the middle; not only raw or only cooked vegetables but some of each. Not only proteins but also carbohydrates and fats. The fat used in cooking is usually enough. For carbohydrates, choose not candy but unrefined grains and fruits. For proteins, choose first the ones which digest easily: yogurt, soft cheese, eggs, fish and chicken. If you are a vegetarian make sure you know how to combine foods to create complete protein. Don't push yourself; your appetite will increase as your body adjusts to its new function. Watch the baby's response and you will gradually discover the foods which agree best with you and your baby.

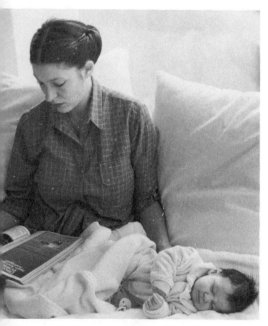

Sleep with your baby close—in your arms, on your chest or next to you in your bed or in a separate container. Now when the baby wakes up you don't need to get up, nor does your baby need to call you by crying. You have noticed its stirring and you check what it needs. Maybe it just needs to be touched and patted a little. Maybe it needs a change in location or position; it could be too warm or too cold, or it needs to burp up some air. Sometimes a gas pain disturbs it, or hunger. If it seems to be the latter, put it to the breast without changing the diaper first. To an infant, hunger is pain and a wet diaper is not as urgent as filling the stomach. Also, suckling often releases bladder and bowels again.

Observe the nursing interaction between you. Is the baby's body fully relaxed against yours? Is its head supported in alignment with its body? Can it take a rest from suckling without the threat of losing the nipple? Is it able to breathe through its nose? If not, indent the breast to make a little breathing path.

If a baby squirms and complains and lets go of the nipple, then grasps it again, it is probably bothered by air which needs to be burped up or be released as gas. Hold the baby up to help the bubble rise. If no burp occurs and the baby roots for the breast again, let it go back to nursing, because suckling changes the tension in the intra-abdominal muscles and thus eases the release of gas and other bowel content.

While you allow the baby to use the breast for its various needs, do not permit misuse. Its attachment to the breast should always be correct: if the baby pulls more on one side of the nipple, the resulting extra wear might create soreness there. While the baby is an infant, support both breast and baby in alignment so the nipple goes straight into the baby's mouth. One of the infant's hands should be below, the other above the breast. As your infant matures, it will caress and hold the breast while gazing at you. Nature placed woman's breasts so that baby and mother can look at each other during nursing. When the baby gets stronger, it can suckle without your close attention and without your holding your breast. Then you can read if you like while nursing, or continue some other activity which requires only one hand.

PAINFUL SWELLING OF THE BREASTS

Even though the free suckling of the baby may lessen the initial swelling of the breasts, some engorgement will probably occur on the second or third day. If the breasts become painfully swollen and hard, soften them in warm water before nursing. Fill a very clean bowl with hot water. Wash the hands with soap and smooth them with a few drops of oil. Place the bowl in front of your body on a table or the sink and lean forward to submerge one breast in the warm water. Cup your hands at the base of your breast and slide them toward your nipple gently at first, then with firmer strokes. If there is an area which feels especially hard, massage it with extra care. A clogged duct usually opens to a massaging hand. When the breast feels softer, lift it out of the water and try to express some fluid to further relieve tension. Treat the other breast then let the baby nurse.

A bra with a snug fit may make you more comfortable too. However, if your breasts are so large that none of your bras fit don't think you need to send for a bra with a larger cup, because this engorgement will not last more than twenty-four hours. Some women say a warm heating pad on the breasts a few minutes before nursing and crushed ice applied after each feeding helped them through the engorgement period.

If in spite of this treatment the breasts, including the area around the nipples, remain hard, be extra careful with nursing. Position baby and breast well. If the baby cannot get a proper hold of the dark part of the nipple, use a breast shield. Place this plastic nipple over your own. The baby's sucking on it will cause suction on the breast and the fluid will be released. Between nursings relieve the discomfort by standing under a warm shower, by using hot wet towels on the breasts or, if they remain painful pack them with crushed ice, but not for too long because ice and tight binding of the breasts are used to prevent the milk from coming in. Discontinue the use of the breast shield as soon as the breasts soften—usually within twenty-four hours. Now watch the baby's suckling tech-

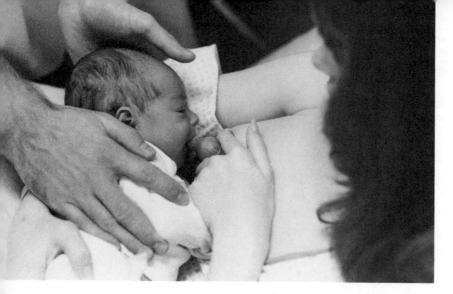

nique carefully again because the breast shield may have taught it a method not quite correct for the breast. The nipple should be between its tongue and palate and its gums should massage the areola. The pull on the nipple is evenly distributed.

CARE OF THE NIPPLES

To help the nipples adjust to their new function, air them well after nursing. Expose them carefully to some sunlight if you can. A nipple cream or hydrous lanolin may help too. Soreness in one area means that spot somehow gets overworked. Give the nipple a slight twist just as the baby takes it into its mouth. Now the extra friction will not rub the same spot again. The sore spot will heal faster when exposed to air and when the circulation to the sore is improved. Some women use warm air from a hand-held hair dryer, others the heat from a light bulb, after each feeding. Should the sore change into a small wound, help it heal by using heat and cold. Gently stroke the wound with an ice cube, then blow on it with the warm air from a hair dryer. Repeat a few times and finish with dry heat. Such a tiny wound is excruciatingly painful those first moments when the baby takes the nipple, then it lessens. If the pain remains intense, the baby is probably not suckling correctly. Try to muster the courage to take the baby off the breast by breaking the suction. Then start over. If the suckling remains painful, see if a breast shield helps while the nipple heals.

Your nipples don't need to be washed before or after nursing. The cleaning they get from a daily bath or shower is enough. But those first days it is a good idea to wash the hands regularly with soap, especially before they touch the nipples or the baby's mouth, because the breasts are prone to infection while they adjust to their new function and your body is still recovering from birth. While the breasts do not need to be washed before or after nursing, they should be washed after they have been emptied if milk was leaking in anticipation of nursing. Soap is fine on the breast skin, but for the nipple and the areola, plain water is better.

PREVENTING A BREAST INFECTION

The breasts are most liable to infection while they adjust to their new function or when the body's overall resistance is lessened by tension and fatigue. Rest, cleanliness, good nutrition and close observation are the best prophylaxis. The first manifestation of a beginning infection is often a localized tender swelling. Therefore continue to massage your breasts daily with strokes from the base to the nipple and with rotation of the flat hand against the full breasts and the chest. If you detect a lump, lift your breast, then massage the lump, stroking toward the nipple. Watch the area where the lump is while the baby nurses. Make sure it is not sagging to the side or in some other way hindered from emptying itself. Lift it to make it part of the breast and massage it toward the nipple. Rest as much as possible and drink lots of fluids, especially water. Keep an eye on your temperature. If you have a fever of .5° above normal an antibiotic may be necessary. The pediatrician will know which one will attack the infection without hurting the baby. An infection caught at the start is rarely a reason to interrupt nursing. Rest, fluid and foods which are digested easily allow antibiotics their full effect. Yogurt can help the bowels restore the bacteria which are essential for their functioning but were wiped out by the antibiotic. Do take the full course of antibiotics the physician prescribes even though pain and temperature disappear the first day. If you don't, the infection will probably flare up again and this time the bacteria may be resistant to that antibiotic.

SUPPORTING THE NURSING MOTHER

The initial secretions of the breasts are yellowish, then they become watery white. The milk for human offspring is different from that for goats or for cows, but the mother in her anxiety worries that hers is not rich enough. Yet the baby loves its sweet taste and flourishes on its particular combination of essential nutrients. The antibodies in mother's milk help the baby combat infection.

As a father who watches this process and reflects on the difference between mothering and fathering, maybe you can extend the traditional role of fathering, not by wanting a breast or by giving the baby formula, but by supporting your wife in what only her body can do—making food especially for this baby. When she has doubts, remind her that her body was able to support the baby's growth quite well so far. After all, the baby is lovely, is it not? She may also wonder whether she has enough milk. The number of wet diapers is a good indication. Six per day usually means the baby drinks enough. Bowel movements count too. A baby who gets enough milk usually has a few messy diapers per day. Also, take into ac-

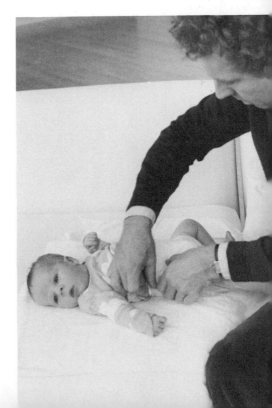

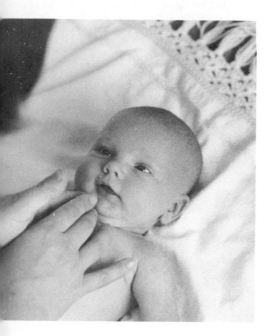

count the baby's overall behavior. Crying over a burp ceases with the sound of one. Crying over gas is as intermittent as the cramps, and in general, crying over pain ceases when the pain is relieved. And hunger pain is only relieved by food. So if the baby does not stop crying after nursing, and if it has few wet diapers and bowel movements, it may not be getting enough milk. Help your wife rest more, bring her plenty of fluids to drink and ease her worries. Do not resort to formula until the pediatrician (whom you have chosen partly because of his enthusiasm for nursing) agrees with you that a supplement is necessary. A supplement will lessen the amount of suckling on the breasts and therefore the milk production, and formula, while an adequate substitute for mother's milk, is of lower quality.

New mothers have always worried over the quality and quantity of their milk, from the times when the only alternative to nursing was a wet nurse, which meant the mother had to give up a lot of her time with the baby. Formula is a much more acceptable solution, but many mothers, insecure in their new function, resort to it too soon. At the Breast Feeding Clinic of the Los Angeles County Hospital new mothers who cannot afford bus fare come by foot with their babies, because they too worry about their milk. Some, too poor to own a sweater for a cold day, buy formula while their breasts overflow. They think that the bottle and formula given them by the midwife or nurse who attended them through childbirth is superior, and like any mother, they want nothing but the best for their children.

A new mother needs a person who cares about her and believes in her. This person does not need to be there all day long, just every once in a while when she is worn out or loses perspective or forgets about herself in her overwhelming concern for the new and precious life. Help your wife with your presence and your understanding but make your help practical as well. Make sure that her position during nursing is such that it causes the least amount of tension and fatigue. In bed she should sit up or be on her side. If she chooses the sitting position, her body should be well supported against the wall or against a backrest with pillows. A pillow or two in her lap allows her to rest the arm which holds the baby. One under the thighs will raise her lap and stabilize the pelvis so she can relax. If her spine is strong and her pelvic region flexible, the semi-lotus position will be excellent. If not, a chair with arms and a footstool is better. Extra pillows might help to support the arm holding the baby. No matter how comfortable the position of nursing, her upper back will become tired and tense. Massage it with firm hands the way you know helps her best. And bring her something to drink, put on a favorite record or read to her. Then maybe you can burp and change the baby while she does a few stretches to relieve the tension in her upper back.

Mother's milk usually leaves the baby's stomach within two hours and an empty stomach causes hunger pains. So even after a good meal the baby will ask for food again before long. Also, because the breast is its comfort and security in this strange new world, the baby will not like nursing to be limited to twenty minutes every three hours. It likes to be listened to, understood and accepted. And it needs to grow. So let the baby nurse as much as it wants. Don't worry, it will gradually grow away from the breast. At day ten, it can be away from it for a little while but not usually for more than two hours, often less. But between three and four months, it is likely to go for three and four hours in the day and eight to twelve at night without asking to nurse. Now the fourth trimester is over. The baby is ready to look at the world and itself. Until then it has been preoccupied mostly with internal functioning. The demands on a new mother are very heavy at this time, but by paying such close attention to the baby's needs she will actually be giving it a firmer base from which to develop independence later on, so with her own growing understanding and the support of her husband or friend, she can give to her baby as much as it needs during this intimate period.

THE RELIEF BOTTLE: YOUR OWN MILK OR FORMULA

At birth a baby will take either breast or bottle, but at two months a baby who never had a bottle before has formed a definite preference for the breast. The bottle to such a baby is a ridiculous-feeling and -tasting thing for which it has no use and which it will not take. It would rather wait for the breast. Thus a mother who has to return to a job where she cannot bring her infant should raise her child on breast and bottle.

Do wait to introduce the bottle until breast feeding is well established. This means the engorgement is past, the milk is in, and there are no sore nipple problems and you are confident that your milk is okay. This often takes about two weeks. Empty the breasts manually after a feeding and store the milk in the refrigerator. When about four ounces have been accumulated offer them in a bottle at room temperature to the baby. Cleanliness is very important because milk spoils easily. Wash bottle and nipple very well. Also wash your hands and the container in which the milk is collected with soap and water. Milk keeps for a few hours outside a refrigerator, inside one for twenty-four hours, and in the freezer for one year. But freezing food kills the enzymes, thus making absorption less efficient.

Hold the baby close while it takes the bottle. Should it refuse the plastic nipple, entice it to take it by sweetening the tip with Karo syrup. Support the baby's head comfortably and in alignment with its body and make sure the bottle is held at such an angle that the nipple is filled with milk. Let the baby suckle and rest at its own rhythm, but do hold it up for a burp every once in a while. Babies seem to swallow more air with a bottle than with the breast.

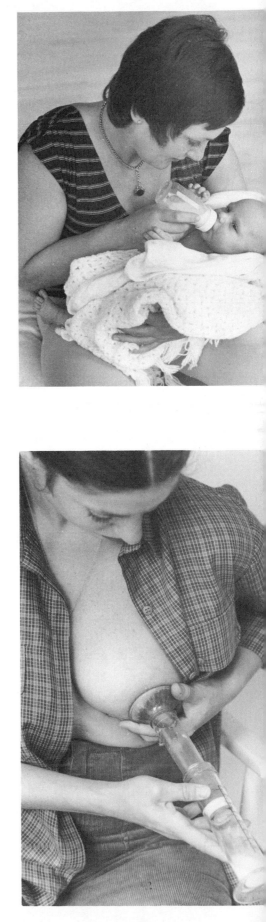

Manual expression of milk appears to be best for the breasts. However, it is a tedious task. Pumps have been invented to speed the process. The manual pumps made by Kaneson and the electric pumps by Egnell are both excellent. The latter might be available on a rental basis. Check with an agency which rents out medical equipment or with the local chapter of the LaLeche League, an international organization which assists nursing mothers.

Some working women can go home for lunch, others leave milk behind and pump their breasts at work, saving it there in the refrigerator to take home for the next day. I know women judges and women janitors who took care of their babies' nutrition this way. The reason for expressing milk from the breasts instead of giving formula is simply one of nutrition—breast milk is for most babies the best food. There are fewer allergies and digestive problems in breast-fed babies than in those given formula. Formula should be reserved for cases of inadequate supply or for the very rare baby who is allergic to milk.

TOO MUCH OR NOT ENOUGH MILK

The ejection of milk, which at first happens only while nursing, becomes soon a more easily triggered reflex. In some mothers the thought of the baby makes the milk flow. Some are warned by a tingling feeling, and say that immediate pressure applied with the palm of the hand on the nipple prevents the release of milk. If no such warning occurs or if this technique does not stop the milk from flowing, wear a comfortable bra with disposable or washable pads to catch the milk. Handkerchiefs work fine. They can be washed and they don't fall apart after soaking up fluid. Some mothers prefer breast protectors, containers which fit the breast and catch the milk. Do not add this milk to your stored supply if it accumulated slowly at body temperature. When you dress up to go out you won't have to worry about leakage if you cut up a mini-pad and place a piece so it covers your nipple and areola. The adhesive on the back will make it stick to the cup of your bra and the plastic will protect your clothes. But do not wear plastic regularly because the resulting lack of air circulation may increase nipple soreness and the chance of infection.

I know of no technique to slow down over-production. In some mothers the abundant flow is too rapid for the baby, who gulps and swallows yet cannot keep up. If possible, empty the breasts a bit before nursing and store this milk for future use or save it for babies of mothers who are less well endowed. You can donate it through the nursery of your local hospital or through your pediatrician. If one breast sprays milk while the baby empties the other, try the palm-of-the-hand technique or catch the milk in a clean cup or a breast protector and add it to the stored supply.

When the breasts have adjusted to their new function, the feeling of fullness disappears. Now the mother worries again, "Do I still have enough?" Look at your baby. If its skin fits it nicely, it appears to be growing and it urinates regularly, there is no need to worry about quantity or quality. If there is evidence that the supply is diminishing—the baby cries at the breast and when it lets go of the nipple manual extraction produces no milk—realize that the recipe to increase production is still the same: rest, lots of fluids, good nutrition and frequent contact between baby and breast. If you and your pediatrician agree that it is necessary, offer the baby a supplement, but not until it has suckled both breasts. Encourage it to nurse again soon.

Arm exercises improve the flow of blood and lymph and therefore the functioning of the breasts, but neither exercise nor rest, fluid or nutrition will give every mother enough milk. They do, however, give a slightly inadequate supply the best chance at improving.

OTHER PROBLEMS WITH NURSING

The nursing behavior of each baby is as unique as all the other qualities that make it an individual. Some babies continue to refuse a bottle no matter how tactfully it is introduced to them. Others, who were given formula before nursing was well established, adamantly refuse the breast. Some prefer one breast over the other. The left is more often favored than the right. In such a case, give the less favorite one first some of the time, then let the baby take dessert from the one it likes better. If a baby con-

tinually and adamantly refuses one breast yet takes the other, have the rejected breast examined by a specialist to make sure there is no cancer or other hidden disease. If the baby likes both breasts, alternate the first breast at each feeding until nursing is well established. Then it is no longer necessary to offer both breasts every time unless this makes the breasts feel more comfortable.

Even in infancy, a baby's opinion can be hard to change. If it is, respect seems the only response, difficult as it may be, especially when the mother has milk and is convinced nursing is better yet the baby refuses the breast. Maybe nursing is not always better. It certainly is not always possible. While the inability to produce sufficient milk occurs infrequently, there are women whose breasts do not cooperate. No milk, continuous soreness of the nipples, a burning pain inside the breasts during nursing which does not get better after a few days, or extreme proneness to infection are among the known problems. If such a problem presents itself, you, the obstetrician and the pediatrician may agree, however reluctantly, that you should discontinue nursing. The decision may well be difficult to accept. Deep feelings do not seem to be governed by reason, but try to overcome your feelings of failure and disappointment by being rational. Allow the feeling to arise, then speak back to it: "Yes, I would have liked to nurse. Of course I tried. I did what I could. Fortunately the baby does well with my care on formula. I did not fail my baby. My breasts just could not nurse. But while my breasts failed, my mothering is successful. Breast feeding is only a part of mothering, and the most important mothering is to guide someone helpless toward independence."

WEANING

When one member of the family of father, mother and baby feels that it is time to stop, it may be time for weaning. How this is done will depend on the circumstances as well as the age and temperament of the baby. An occasional baby decides that it is time to stop and simply refuses the breast. But most prefer to be weaned slowly.

Leave out the baby's least favorite nursing time first, such as the one after the mashed fruit in the morning. When the breasts begin to make less milk, leave out the next one, until finally only the one at bedtime remains. Now think about it for a few days. Is it really time to stop? If it is but your baby cannot quite let go, offer it a bottle and hold it close so it knows it is not losing you, or sucking, but only the breast. Some women prefer to have someone else put the baby to bed for a few nights. The breasts will be swollen and sore. Bind them close to the body with a bra or with a thin towel pinned around the chest. Use crushed ice if the swelling is painful. Within twenty-four hours the milk production will stop, then the fluid will be reabsorbed and the body will return to a non-lactating state.

Part Six

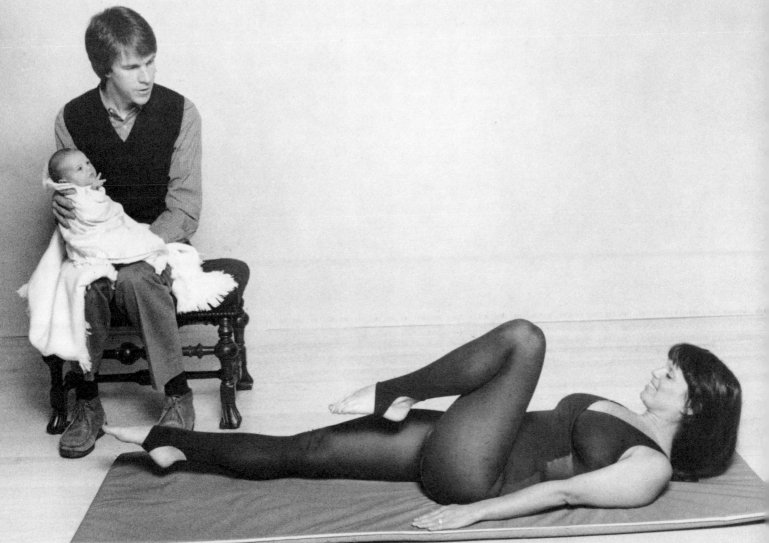

Recovery & the Recovery Workout:
SKILLS & EXERCISES

ON RECOVERY
IN GENERAL

I believe that it is not until conception and birth that a woman truly loses her virginity. A woman is never quite the same after becoming a mother as she was before; she sheds what remains of her adolescent, nymphlike, carefree nature. This transformation is vastly appealing to all but an immature and demanding male. The man who has become a father looks at his wife's devotion to their delicate offspring with a fondness deeper than anything they had shared before.

Recovery, like growth, proceeds in a spiral; there is a pause, even some receding before each step forward. Thus after a good day there may well be one where you feel like doing nothing. It's okay to indulge yourself then and rest, so the next day can be better again. A healing wound, whether in the lower abdomen or near the vagina, remains sensitive for a while, and with fatigue this sensitivity changes to pain. Exhaustion follows quickly on the heels of mild fatigue during convalescence, and exhaustion, especially at the start of the seemingly never-ending and overwhelming task of motherhood, makes you susceptible to melancholy, gloom and irritability. So take good care of yourself; respect the first signs of fatigue, and rest.

Your emotional recovery will follow a similar spiral pattern; the initial delight with the baby may be followed by a strange sense of loss which is then succeeded by a new surge of joy. Bend gracefully with these changes of feeling, they are a quite natural part of your growth as a woman and mother.

Even if labor was prolonged and exhausting, many new mothers experience an energy rush and aren't able to rest right after the birth. Body and mind are filled with a new tension. There is an urge to begin to take care of oneself and the baby. I wonder if it is a remnant of an earlier time when a woman had to take care of her infant, its cord and the afterbirth, as well as herself.

Among peoples with more primitive technology, it was customary for a new mother to submerge herself (sometimes with infant in arms) in the bathing hole of the nearby stream. After an uncomplicated birth, it is perfectly safe for you to get up, stretch your legs, go to the bathroom and take a shower as soon as you feel ready. If a prolonged labor, spinal anes-

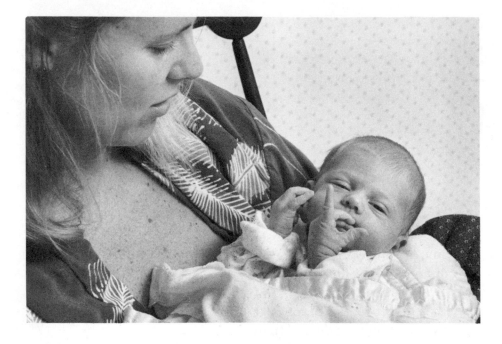

thesia, a large episiotomy or more extensive surgery delay your ability to take care of yourself, a sponge bath with a light massage will feel like a real treat. Once thus refreshed and with the baby close by, you will be able to rest.

The main organ in the drama of birth heals by its own efforts. In the weeks following birth, the uterus contracts itself back to a small pear-shaped organ in the lower abdomen while the area where the placenta was attached is restored. The regenerating cells secrete fluid. First an abundant flow of fresh red blood appears at the vagina, then a few days later the flow slows down to take on the brownish color of old blood. Next a mucus-like lymph adds itself, changing the color to pink. And when all bleeding ceases, the discharge may become almost white with an occasional unexplained flare-up of some bleeding. This post-birth discharge, called lochia, stops when the healing is complete, usually between three and six weeks. The smell of lochia is the same as that of the fluid secreted by all healing cells, and because of the location will somewhat resemble the smell of a period. When color or smell depart from this, contact your midwife or physician. Sometimes a small piece of the membranes has remained attached to the uterine lining, causing a flare-up of profuse bleeding or the discharge of pieces of tissue. If you have a bacterial infection you will have a more odorous flow. Like any wound, this one in the uterus is susceptible to infection. Therefore as long as a discharge is present, nothing should enter the vagina; no sexual intercourse and no tampons to catch the fluid. While you are up and about wear a sanitary napkin. When at rest you should, some of the time, allow the entrance to the vagina to air by placing a towel or a disposable pad under the buttocks to catch the fluid.

For each pregnancy you have, the strength with which the uterus is able to contract seems to increase. Therefore contractions during second and subsequent pregnancies are noted earlier and seem more pronounced; those of labor expel the child faster; and those of recovery, painless with the first child, can be painful for a few hours after the birth of subsequent children.

Since nipple stimulation releases oxytocin (the hormone which helps milk ducts empty and makes the uterus contract), nursing can cause painful contractions. It will also temporarily increase the flow of lochia, but it speeds up the healing process.

During the hours immediately following birth, the uterus occasionally refuses to contract and profuse bleeding results. That is why it is customary to keep a new mother under close observation for a few hours. During this time a nurse or midwife will regularly check both the amount of flow and the muscular tension in the womb. For the latter, the hand is placed on the lower abdomen to feel for the receding uterus, which should now be about the size and shape of a cantaloupe. If the nurse cannot feel it immediately, she can stimulate the flabby womb into contracting with a firm massage. Sometimes administration of synthetic oxytocin is necessary to make the organ return to work.

RECOVERY FROM A VAGINAL BIRTH

A vaginal birth can temporarily traumatize the area between the legs and make it sore from overstretching. The muscles around the vagina occasionally tear, or if the birth attendant noticed their tightness, they may have been cut to prevent such tearing. The muscles around the bladder opening sometimes respond to the stretch with a temporary inability to relax, and for a few hours, sometimes longer, a new mother may have difficulty letting go of urine. Around the rectum the stretch quite often causes a painful localized swelling called hemorrhoids. The occurrence of these problems is not only related to the size of the baby but to the mother's structure, to her control over expulsive efforts and to the skill of the birth attendant as well. Some women deliver a ten-pound baby without soreness, tear or episiotomy.

The initial swelling response can be reduced during the hours which immediately follow birth by applying to the affected area crushed ice in a plastic bag wrapped in a towel. After a good icing, intermittent local application of heat further improves healing. The heat does not need to come from a heat lamp; just the warmth from a light bulb will do.

If difficulty in emptying the bladder continues, the nurse can always help with a catheter. Such catheterization is a simple non-painful procedure in a woman. A nurse gently opens the labia, washes the area in between with cotton balls soaked in a disinfectant, then slips a thin tube into the opening to the bladder to help the urine flow out. Control over this muscle comes back with time, usually within hours after birth.

Stitches between vagina and rectum are made with a material which dissolves. Pain from these stitches is as variable as people's response to pain in general. Some women report no pain at all, others are afraid to move for a few days. The wound itself is usually tender to touch. It will heal best when kept dry, clean and exposed to air. To wash it, use a squirt bottle with warm water, gently open the labia and aim along, not at, the vagina. Dry the general area with a clean towel and let air dry the wound itself. Warm air will do this quicker, either from a light bulb or a hand-held hair dryer. In using the dryer, aim along, not at, the vagina so no air is blowing in.

Hemorrhoids will also heal faster with intermittent use of heat. Submerge just this region in warm water with Epsom salts. When the hemorrhoids soften, massage them gently to help the rectal tissue release the blood which caused the swelling.

Stitches and hemorrhoids can make sitting quite painful. It is tempting to sit on a foam rubber ring which allows the painful area to float free. This is fine for dinner and other occasions, but not all the time; because the localized pressure interferes with the circulation to the rectum and therefore slows the healing of the hemorrhoids. Rest frequently on your side rather than sitting or reclining. And at regular intervals assume the knee-chest position, which relieves all pressure on this area and therefore improves circulation.

Exercise the muscles in between the legs by gently tightening and releasing them in rhythmic repetitions. The movement is similar to stopping the flow of urine. Increase the number of repetitions slowly and also the length of time you can hold the muscles tight. It takes time for these muscles to become strong and efficient again. Aim first for ten repetitions, holding each tightening for one second, and try to do a few groups of ten per day. Continue the discipline of working the pelvic floor with this so-called Kegel exercise for at least half a year. Work up to twenty-four repetitions twice a day.

Avoid standing for long periods and heavy lifting while the uterus is enlarged and the supporting pelvic muscles are stretched. Squat or kneel down to caress another child rather than lifting it up to you. Sit down or walk holding your baby but don't stand for any length of time.

RECOVERY FROM A CESAREAN SECTION

The human body heals faster after childbirth than at any other time. Even the recovery from a cesarean section is amazingly fast. There is more pain after an abdominal delivery and in a different region, but the healing of the uterus is the same, so lochia will still pass through the vagina.

Following the removal of baby and placenta, both the uterus and the abdominal muscles are carefully stitched with a material which slowly dissolves. Only the stitches in the skin may be the kind which need removing. All stitching is done with such care that were it not for the pain, one could move about immediately after surgery without fear of a rupture. But I think the initial microscopic healing may be helped by the immobilization which post-surgical pain tends to impose for a few hours or a day.

During this initial healing phase, you should clear your lungs well at regular intervals by doing breathing exercises and protect the circulation of your legs from too much inactivity. Unfortunately the physical therapy which specializes in helping people recover from surgery has barely touched the surgery of childbirth, yet it is here that a fast recovery is most desirable. Also the nurses on a postpartum ward are not as geared toward assisting a surgical patient as those on the surgical wards. Therefore, your partner and coach can be a great help.

As a coach, stay only if you feel up to it and can give your help to the new mother freely. If it makes her feel obliged to carry on a conversation, to look better than she feels or to worry about your fatigue, she is better off by herself while you recover your strength at home. Maybe a close friend, sister or mother can take your place for a while.

Be prepared for her complaints about pain as she dozes off and wakes up. Use your voice in a caressing and encouraging manner: "The pain will let up soon. Maybe you need a little more pain relief. There is nothing wrong with using it today. Tomorrow you will need much less of it because the pain will be so much less." Keep her lips moist and when she is allowed fluids, help her drink by holding the glass and letting her sip from a bent straw so she does not have to raise her head, because lifting the head is done partially with the abdominal muscles. When you stroke sweaty hair out of the way or turn her pillow over, lift her head for her, but only slightly, and support it well.

If her bed is not the adjustable kind where the back can be raised and the knees lifted, place a pillow under her thighs for short intervals. This slight bending of the knees releases tension in the pelvic region.

Don't be afraid of what you might see when you swing the blanket back and her gown is not covering her. The stitches in the skin will be covered with a small dressing. The clean shaven pubic region reveals its triangular form. A catheter will be visible from in between the labia. It stays in the bladder because at its tip is a small balloon which was filled with a sterile fluid after the catheter was inserted. The resulting increase in diameter prevents it from slipping out until the balloon is emptied. Should this balloon press on the area where the urethra leaves the bladder, it will give

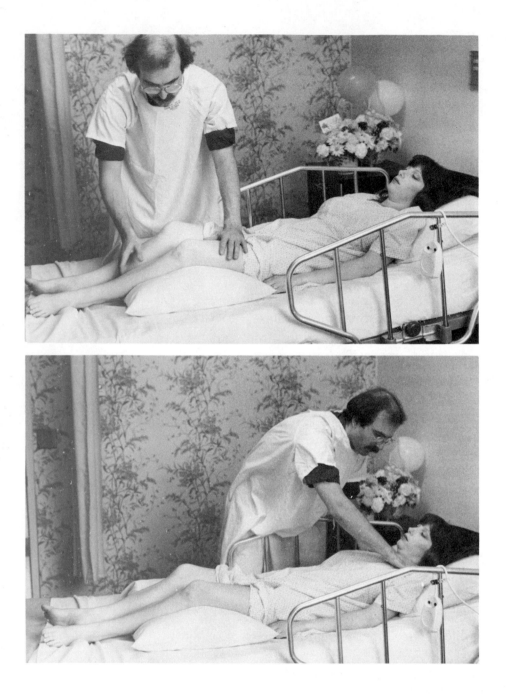

the sensation of a full bladder. To prevent this painful feeling, the catheter is taped against the inside of the leg with a loop. If you inadvertently pull on this loop while helping her move, it can cause her pain. If she complains, take the catheter between clean fingers a few inches away from where it disappears in between the labia and push it in gently a tiny bit.

If she seems up to it, help her practice some chest breathing and panting every couple of hours. She might want to cup her hands over her lower abdomen to protect it from unintentional movement. Put your hands on her ribs and suggest that she expand them well with an inhalation and to let them relax when she exhales. After four to five good breaths, ask her to switch to panting. Suggest that she make the exhalation a little forceful then let the air rush back in. Rub the muscles at the top of her shoulders a bit as well as those along the neck, and stroke her forehead. Then suggest that she rotate her feet at the ankles. If she thinks she can't, do it for her. Gently support the ankle just off the bed and with your other hand rotate the foot. After a few circles with each foot, ask her to slide her legs up and down a few times alternating them slowly without lifting them. Then let her doze off to sleep.

If the nurse can put a cot in her room for you, you might want to rest off and on too, especially if you helped her with a long labor. If you are not too tired and your baby is fine, consider caring for it. Suggest to the nurse in charge that it be brought to the mother as if she were able to care for it and say, "I will do the caring." The nurse should be able to answer any questions which arise about caring for your baby in the hospital. If you like, you can sit or lie down next to your wife with your baby in your arms. You can offer it water if it seems eager to suckle, or if the mother feels up to it, you can let it nurse.

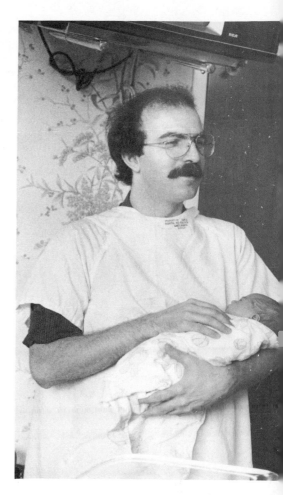

Raise the back of her bed a little and bend it a bit at the knees or place a pillow under the thighs. Loosen her gown and bring it down over her shoulder to expose one or both breasts. Place your baby with its tummy across her chest so its mouth is close to the exposed nipple. Lift the breast with your fingers on one side and your thumb on the other side of the areola and stroke the nipple over the baby's lips. If it opens its mouth, help it take the nipple, then indent the breast to make a little breathing hole for the baby's nose.

If your wife is able to sit up more she might like to hold the baby in her arms. Place a pillow in her lap so the arm which holds the baby can rest. If she is more comfortable in a side-lying position, give her a pillow in between the legs, or if she prefers to have the bottom leg straight, have her fold the top one over on a pillow. Place the baby in her arm closest to the bed. This arm is bent at the elbow to fold down along her body to encircle the infant, while the upper arm and hand are free to manipulate the breast.

If your presence is helpful to your wife and being there is rewarding to you, consider spending the night. Maybe the baby can stay with the two of you instead of in the newborn nursery.

The second day after an operation most people feel much better. Yet the nurse's announcement that it is time to get out of bed seems at first a bit much. Work up to it slowly. First try some deep breaths. Cup your hands over your lower abdomen and inhale carefully, letting your abdomen expand first, then your chest. Let the air flow out without contracting

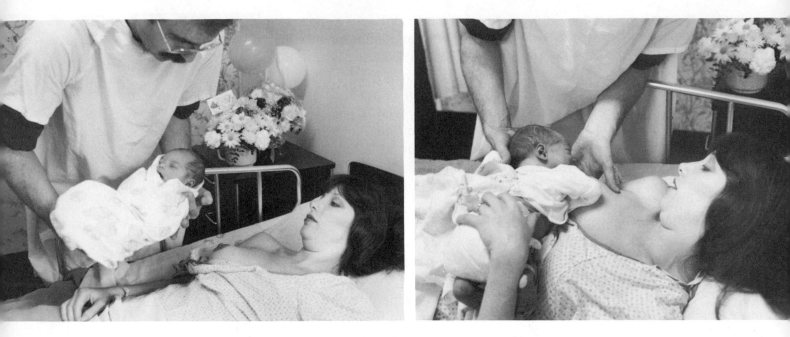

your abdominal muscles. Next rotate your ankles and then slide your legs up and down a few times. Roll your head from side to side and make a few big circles with your shoulders. Then turn on your side and slowly and carefully swing your legs over the edge of the bed and push your upper body up with your arms. Adjust to being upright and self-supported for a few moments, then dangle your legs a bit before you place them on the footstool. Support yourself on the edge of the bed or with your arms on the nurse's shoulders when you shift your weight onto your legs. Keep your knees slightly bent and let your upper body round forward a bit. Shift your weight to one leg and step down from the footstool with the other. Shift the weight on this one and bring the second leg down. Place your hands over your lower abdomen and straighten up as much as possible, then walk with little steps to the armchair. Turn your back to the seat of this chair with the back of your legs touching the edge of the seat. Place your hands on the arms of the chair, and let them bear most of your weight when you lower yourself slowly.

Take your time for this adventure of getting up the first time. Try not to hold your breath during these efforts and don't tense muscles which need not be involved in the work. When you get up out of the chair, use your arms and your thighs to push yourself up. Rise slowly and, now that you know you can move about again, choose with care each movement that will help you get back in bed.

The catheter may be removed before you are ready to get up to use the bathroom, so you may need to use a bedpan. After abdominal surgery, getting on a bedpan is harder from an upright position than from an al-

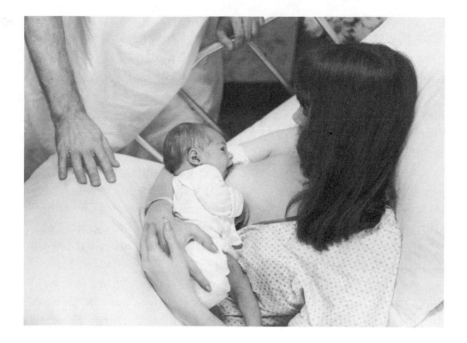

most flat one. The movement one makes to get on the bedpan is an exaggerated pelvic rock—actually a fine recovery exercise. Practice it a few times before having to put it into practice with a full bladder.

Lie on your back with your feet hip distance apart, your knees bent and your hands cupped over your lower abdomen. Inhale, then while you exhale, press your lower back into the bed to tilt the area between the legs upward. Slowly tuck, release, tuck, and release the pelvis a few times and with the discovery that this rocking does not add to the pain, increase the range of movement by lifting the buttocks just off the bed while the lower back continues to press the bed underneath. Repeat a few times.

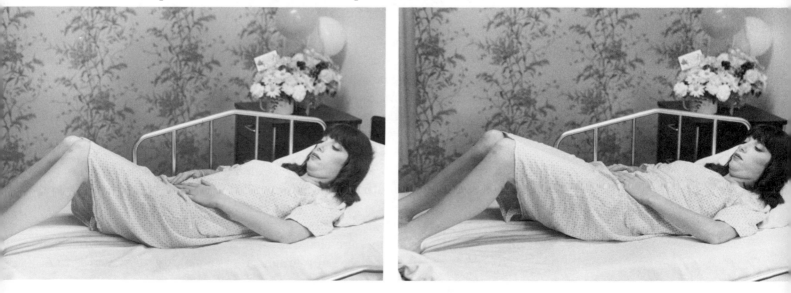

To slide a bedpan under you, you may need to raise the buttocks a little farther than when doing this exercise. Do it slowly and carefully, always with the image of reaching with your lower back toward the bed rather than letting it arch up. Keep your shoulder blades on the bed. Once the bedpan is placed, the nurse can help you get more upright by raising the back of your bed or by letting you push yourself up with your arms while she lifts your upper body.

The third day following abdominal surgery, the bowels will register their protest at having been disturbed. These gas pains are relieved in some women by walking, in others by resting on the left side with the top leg bent on a pillow to further relax the abdominal muscles. In severe cases, the nurse may be able to help with a Harris flush. Through a catheter in the rectum warm water is flooded into the bowels and as it leaves, it takes the air in its path.

When recovery is well on its way and the crisis is over, there is energy for reflection again. Many feelings arise, and among them may be those of disappointment and sadness. Some women feel almost forlorn. The psyche has its own healing to do after an operation and after this one, which stopped a process for which it had become programmed by pregnancy, the upheaval can be quite painful. Don't be afraid of a good cry when it comes. Accept the regret that you could not give birth the way you had hoped and the resentment that it is taking so long to feel well again. Only then can you feel grateful that you and your baby came through it well, even though by a different route. Whether or not you will need a cesarean for a subsequent birth depends on the reason for the surgery. A narrow pelvis will remain narrow, but a loop in the cord or a breech position usually won't recur, so you may well be able to enjoy a vaginal birth the next time.

NEW PERCEPTIONS

Recovery coincides with assuming life as the mother of an infant and is therefore a challenging task because your own body needs care while you are caring for a helpless being whose needs never end. Your new task, with its numerous unexpected interruptions and the resulting exhaustion, may make you feel disorganized. Let your bed be your headquarters and keep the baby and the necessities for its care within easy reach.

The circumstances of the lives of new mothers vary considerably of course, and many of us tend to envy women with big houses, partners, relatives, servants and nanny. But the essential ingredient for healing and motherhood lies within each of us. It is the dignity to live one's own life and make it as good as it can be. As a parent, your child will learn more from you than from anyone else how to live. It learns not from what you say, but from who you are. Your actions are the melody of what it is to be

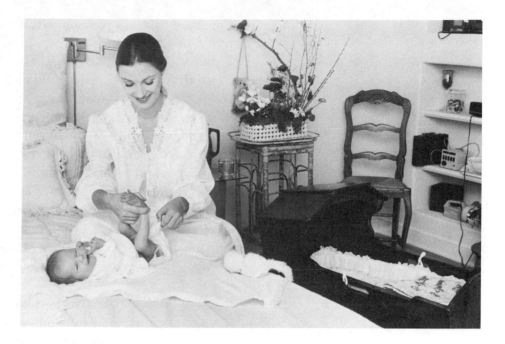

human and you. Be both cautious and courageous, and your child will flourish from the example of your balance and strength. Those gifts are far more important than any material gifts you will ever give your child. So do your best to face up to your new responsibilities and to enjoy the love and help of people you know you can depend on.

Be as realistic as possible about the circumstances of your own life. Don't continue to rely on people who have made a habit of letting you down. If you are alone, enjoy your independence. If you are married, share where possible with your partner. Each arrangement has its own joys and problems. Accept yours, and let them enrich your new life.

Don't be afraid of the many new feelings which may surge to the surface and at times throw you off balance. After the initial rapture at the child's perfection and fear that neither you nor the world may be good enough for it, will come days of delight in the child's growth as well as moments of frustration and despair when the baby keeps on crying in spite of your best efforts. There is fatigue and weariness too, during those first weeks. And resentment at times that being a mother is as difficult as it is, and awe at the amount of love it will take to help this baby become the person it was meant to be. There may be fear that in giving this love you may not be able to let go when the time comes, or that in giving freely to the child there may not be enough for your partner.

During this time of upheaval give some thought to your interactions with loved ones so you may see with greater clarity the difference between love for husband and love for child; the feelings and responsibilities are very different. Mother love is by its nature very protective, yet much of your success as a mother will lie in your ability to pursue your own life.

Continue to share yourself with your lover for conversation, a pleasant activity, or just resting together. It will leave you refreshed as you return to care for the baby.

Your ability to love your child and your lover depends a great deal on another kind of love—your love for yourself, your confidence, your sensitivity, your inner strength, your special light that shimmers in the world and is the wellspring of your existence. Never is access to this source of inner strength more important than when a delicate new being depends on you for its physical and emotional well-being. Use your new perceptions to learn more about yourself. Don't be afraid of the rawness of your feelings: crying and states of ecstasy may follow each other for no apparent reason. Birth has not only changed the hormones, it has also opened to the light of day parts of yourself that are very sensitive. Don't close up. Just be careful to whom you expose these new aspects of yourself.

Take a few moments to be alone here and there when the baby is sleeping or happy with someone else. On a firm pillow sit in semi-lotus position. Make sure the buttocks are pulled back, the midriff is lifted and the crown of the head is extended to the ceiling. Rest your hands on your knees and cast your eyes down along the tip of your nose. Concentrate on your breathing, just on the air flowing in and out, and try not to think at all. Now listen to yourself. Remind yourself you are still the most important being. In the daily routine of things it may seem that the baby is the focus of your life, but don't lose sight of your own importance, your uniqueness as a human being. Deep down, you are as good as you are for your baby out of respect for yourself. And every day you learn a little bit more about caring for yourself by caring for others. A mother does not give herself away. A mother gives of herself and in so doing she enriches herself.

Motherhood is not an easy task. Its initial phase seems most difficult for women who have left a busy and satisfying career and the rhythm of the business world. The inability to "schedule" mothering can produce a bit of culture shock. You may miss the frequent interaction with adults which formed a major part of your days. And even though you are taking good care of your baby, it cannot say, "Thank you, I could not have done it without you." But when your friends discuss their complex interactions and achievements at the end of the day and yours was spent nursing and changing and burping and rocking, don't feel inadequate. You are helping a small person adjust to living on its own. The most tedious phase of this caring will not last very long and you can choose whether you want to have more children later. So give to this baby without fear of losing too much of your own life.

Realize also that difficult is not the same as awful. When something is hard you will succeed when you give it your best. And in giving it your best, the best is brought out of you.

While the relationship between mother and child lies at the very core of the child's development, it is not the only influential one, nor need this crucial human tie be worn thin by over-exposure. Many mothers and children flourish better when they do not have to interact twenty-four hours every day.

SHARING AS PARENTS

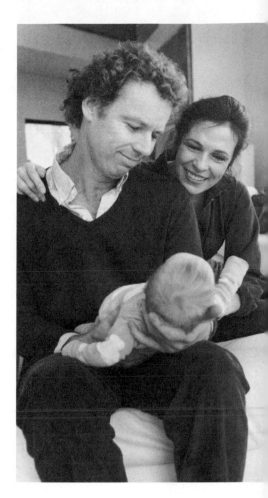

If you are a father who assisted in the baby's birth, you are probably every bit as emotionally involved as a new mother during those first days. You may want to hold your baby often and talk with it, not just to help your wife but because you want to get to know this little person and give it a chance to know you from the start. The role of a father is different but no less important, and the interaction between new parents should be complementary rather than competitive. Your child may learn from the way you help each other about cooperation and sharing.

New parents are of course concerned about being able to provide well for their child. But don't confuse a good life with a wealthy one. It is essential to have some money, and a little extra is pleasant, but the most valuable gifts you can give your child will still be your time, your attention and your love. Don't waste these precious years pursuing wealth in a way that keeps you away from your family. Confucius, reflecting on his life, said that the moments he valued most were those of the late afternoon spent walking down to the river with a few friends and their children.

As parents you have made a permanent connection. Do everything you can to treasure your closeness and treat each other with care and respect. Feelings of love ebb and flow, but affection and respect are usually steadier emotions, and can remain more constant. Your relationship will not end when the strong feelings of love subside temporarily—and they will return again.

A baby sometimes brings out a new wave of love between its parents. There is so much to learn, so much to give and so much to think about and share. Although the physical act of penetration should be delayed until the uterus is healed, it is not necessary to abstain from all sexual expressions of love.

Be aware that quite soon after birth the ovaries may resume their former activity of preparing an egg for release. Nursing tends to repress such ovulation but it does not always prevent it. Therefore discuss with your physician or midwife how you can prevent conception during those weeks after birth when the placental site has healed but your body is not ready for your usual method of birth control. Conception before the mother is ready benefits neither mother, child, family or society.

In a woman who is nursing, sexual arousal often releases some milk, however, there is usually less lubrication of the vagina during intercourse. Occasionally dryness of this sensitive region is severe enough to warrant the use of a lubricating lotion. The muscles surrounding the vagina will at first be more relaxed than normal, and the nerve endings there will receive less stimulation when a man enters. Also, the area around the episiotomy can remain sensitive to pressure for a while. But these are only temporary changes and need not make a woman less sexual, they simply offer lovemaking a new challenge.

The phenomenal hormone change which follows birth affects individual women quite differently, but night sweats are common and so is breaking out in a sweat under tension or while nursing. Some women experience a temporary thinning of their hair. The weight loss at birth is rarely more than fifteen pounds. The remaining pounds are lost at a rate very different from woman to woman. Many will not fit in their pre-pregnancy clothes for six months to a year, yet some are as slender as before within three months. If your body takes a little longer, buy some loose-fitting outfits in which you feel attractive. You will have become more than a little tired of your maternity clothes. Don't push the return to your pre-pregnancy figure for fear of losing your husband. Such fears don't give him much credit for his commitment nor for the complexity of his feelings. He was attracted to you in the beginning for reasons other than your small waist, and the relationship between husband and wife has many more aspects than physical attraction.

I think parents owe each other respect and support, and that love remains a gift. Don't be fearful if the more loving feelings between you seem to come and go: every relationship has its periods of closeness and of greater distance, and yours too will have a rhythm all its own.

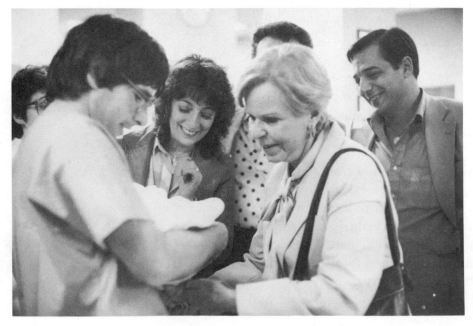

First-time grandmother and other relatives meet the newborn family member, who is wheeled into the waiting room in an isolette to keep her comfortably warm.

THE IMPORTANCE OF GOOD POSTURE

When you begin to move about more, be aware of your posture. The continual pull of the pregnant uterus caused stretching in muscles other than those of the abdomen and this may have altered your ability to stand up straight without effort. Lower back aches are common if the abdominal muscles are weak. Use a footstool or a block not only when you sit in a chair but while standing to do dishes or to change the baby. Place one foot on the footstool without sagging in the other hip, and you will protect your lower back. Watch the way you bend. Squatting down is much safer than bending forward because when your abdominal muscles are weak a forward bend puts too much strain on the lower back.

To help your posture, stand with your back against the wall, then walk your feet out a bit, bend the knees and sit down in an imaginary chair. Your thighs carry the weight and your back is straight against the wall. Place your hands on your abdomen. Inhale, push the belly out. Exhale, pull it in. Make the abdomen move as much as you can. Expand it nicely and pull it in well, keeping every vertebra touching the wall. Hold the pose a little longer every time. Also look in the mirror frequently and each time you notice your belly sticking out because of too great a curve in the lower back, straighten up. Stand and walk tall with the crown of the head reaching straight upward.

THE RECOVERY WORKOUT

While the taboo against exercise in pregnancy has mostly disappeared, some obstetricians continue to impose a long "no exercise" period on women after they give birth. There is no evidence that this is necessary. For the past two years we have seen numerous mothers at Jane Fonda's Workout return to the recovery part of the program when their babies were only two to three weeks old. Those women began to feel better and look better soon after they joined us. I therefore believe it is a good idea to get back in the discipline of exercising as soon as you feel up to it. A cesarean section does not need to keep you from exercising for a long time either. The lower back aches and shoulder tension which can follow abdominal surgery are often relieved when the abdominal muscles become strong again.

Making exercise a routine may be harder now than during your pregnancy because there is so much to do and so little time. Luckily, recovery exercises do not require much time.

The primary aim now is to help the breasts function and relieve tension from nursing, to strengthen the upper body for carrying the baby and its paraphernalia, and to help the pelvic region recover from the stretching of pregnancy and be the center of strength it is designed to be.

Keep in mind that endurance in muscles develops from increasing repetitions of movements without pausing long enough to let the muscles recover. Now that you will rarely be able to count on an hour of uninterrupted time, work for ten minutes or so on one muscle group and do the next important group the next time you have a few minutes. When your baby is awake, place it so you can see each other and count out loud as if you are talking to it. You can do some of the exercises with your baby on top of you or in your arms. It likes movement as much as it did when it was inside you. Remember how it always kicked more when you sat down to rest? Put on a record and sing with the music and you will both have a nice time.

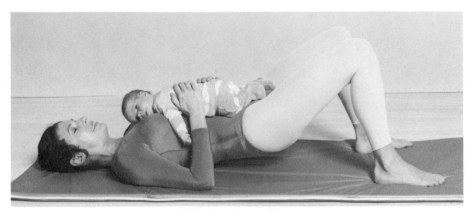

THE UPPER BODY
One CHEST EXPANDER

Starting position: Stand tall, feet hip distance apart, arms lifted to the side and bent at right angles, upper arms parallel to the floor.

Exhale and bring your arms together in front of your chest. Inhale and open them wide. Keep your elbows level with your shoulders. Work up to 24 repetitions.

Two WALL PUSH-UPS

Starting position: Stand tall, slightly more than arm's length away from a wall. Place your feet parallel to each other and hip distance apart. Lean forward and place your palms on the wall slightly below shoulder level, fingers pointing toward the opposite hand.

1. Bring your face to the wall by letting your body come forward as straight as if you had swallowed a ruler, your arms bent at the elbows.

2. Push your body back by straightening your arms. Then come toward the wall again, bending the elbows. Don't leave your buttocks behind and don't let your heels come off the floor. When you are close to the wall you should feel a stretch at your chest and at the back of your legs. If not, place your arms farther apart and/or move your feet a bit farther away from the wall. Repeat 24 times.

Three *THE TOUGH STRETCH*

Starting position: Stand tall with your feet together and parallel. Place the back of your open hands with your little fingers together against your upper back at your shoulder blades.

1. Turn your palms together by bending your elbows back. Maintain the image of extending the crown of your head.

2. Turn your right foot 45° to the right. Step forward with the left foot.

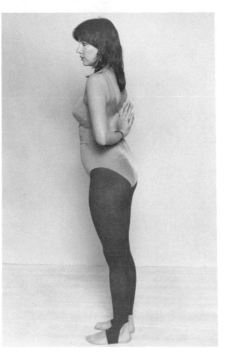

3. Now reach forward with the crown of your head and bend from the hips, keeping your back flat. Watch your breathing and allow your chest, your arms and the backs of your legs to stretch. Keep your elbows up and out to open the chest and ease the pressure at the little fingers.

4. At the point of maximum stretch, drop your head. Hold this position concentrating hard on this difficult stretch, then come up.

Do this exercise again, reversing the position of the legs. If the pain at the little fingers and the wrists is too great, fold the arms behind the back instead of turning the palms together. The stretch in the chest and the opening up of the region of the diaphragm won't be as great but you will achieve the flexibility to keep your palms together with time.

THE PELVIC REGION

The following six exercises are excellent for the first two to three weeks after giving birth:

One LOWER BACK PRESSES

Starting position: Lie on your back with your knees bent and your feet hip distance apart.

Exhale and press your lower back into the floor. Inhale and relax. Work up to 24 repetitions.

Two PELVIC GRIPS

Starting position: Lie on your back with your knees bent and your feet about hip distance apart.

Exhale as you grip and tighten the muscles between the legs—those around the bladder opening, the vagina and the rectum. Inhale and release. Slowly work up to 24 repetitions.

Three RUMP TONERS

Starting position: Lie on your back with your legs straight.

Squeeze your buttocks tight and release. Work up to 24 repetitions.

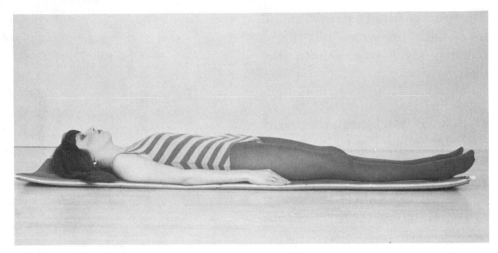

Four EASY CAT STRETCH

Starting position: Kneel on all fours with the weight equally distributed between arms and legs.

1. Exhale, drop head and buttocks under, and pull your back up.
2. Inhale and relax your back to a flat—not sagging—position. Work up to 24 repetitions.

Five CAT TWISTS

Starting position: Kneel on all fours with the arms and thighs forming right angles with the floor.

1. Exhale and turn the right shoulder to the right hip. Inhale, return to center.
2. Exhale, turn the left shoulder to the left hip. Inhale and return to center. Work up to 24 repetitions on each side.

Six CAT STRETCHES

Starting position: Kneel on all fours.
1. Exhale and stretch the left arm and the right leg away from your center. Inhale and put them down.
2. Exhale and repeat the movement to the opposite side. Stretch out with your fingertips and your heel and keep arm and leg parallel to your body. Work up to 48 repetitions, alternating arms and legs.

Once these pelvic exercises can be done without pain or strain, you are ready for more serious work on the abdomen, the buttocks, and the thighs. Finish as many repetitions as you can of each exercise within one session. Do not push too hard, just do a few more repetitions of each exercise every day. If you can find only 10 minutes per day, work one area well rather than trying to squeeze in all three. Then do the next area well the next day.

THE ABDOMEN

In working the abdomen imagine numerous rubber bands, many of them going from the rib cage to the pubic bone and others moving crosswise from the left outer rib cage to the right flank and the right outer rib cage to the left flank. These rubber bands will shorten when you lift the upper body or the legs while lying on your back. But when you shorten them, do it with the image of pulling them inward toward the back rather than letting them bulge out. Scoop the abdomen in while you work it and keep the lower back pressed into the floor.

One *HEAD LIFTS*

Starting position: Lie on your back with your knees bent and your feet slightly more than hip distance apart. Place your hands behind your head (not your neck) with your elbows forward along your face.

Exhale and raise your head; inhale and lower it down, but not quite to where you touch the floor. Exhale up, inhale down. Concentrate on the image of pressing your lower back into the floor with your abdominal muscles whenever you exhale. Gradually work up to 24 repetitions.

Two KNEE-TO-ELBOW LIFTS

Starting position: Lie on your back with your knees bent and your feet slightly more than hip distance apart, your hands folded behind your head.

Exhale and bring one knee and the opposite elbow together. Inhale and put them down. Exhale and bring your other elbow and knee together. Control the movement of each leg. Lift it nicely, let your knee touch your elbow, then put it down.

After 24 repetitions alternating sides, work one side 24 times, then the other side 24 times.

Three EASY KNEE LIFTS

Starting position: Raise yourself into a semi-sitting position, supporting your upper body on your elbows with your hands under your buttocks. Place your feet hip distance apart with your knees bent.

Exhale and bring your knees to your body. Inhale, place your feet on the floor. Exhale, bring your knees in again. Work up to 24 repetitions.

Four ELBOW-TO-KNEE STRETCHES

Starting position: Lying on your back, place your hands behind your head with your elbows forward along your face. Bend your knees, hook your big toes together and let your knees fall open, as close to the body as possible.

1. Exhale and touch your left knee with your right elbow. Inhale and lower your head.

2. Exhale and do the movement to the opposite side. Work up to 24 repetitions on each side.

Five KNEE-TO-CHEST LIFTS

Starting position: Lie on your back with your arms along your body, the left leg straight, the right bent. Lift head and shoulders just off the floor.

1. Bring the right knee to the chest while you stretch the left leg long out of the hip.

2. Alternate legs while the upper body remains lifted. Breathe in short pants in rhythm with the leg movements. Work up to 24 repetitions.

Six KNEE LIFTS

Starting position: Lie on your back and come up on your elbows with your hands under your buttocks. Place the soles of your feet together and let your knees fall open.

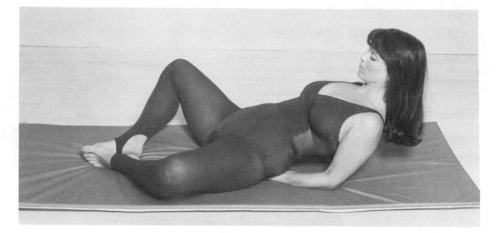

1. Exhale and bring your right knee toward your chest. Inhale, put the foot down.

2. Exhale and bring your other knee toward the chest. You should be able to see your inner thigh when you put your leg down. Lift your knee from that turned-out position. Work up to 24 repetitions.

Seven *SITTING TWISTS*

Starting position: Sit up with your feet on the floor more than hip distance apart, your hands behind your head.

1. Exhale and bring your right elbow and your left knee together. Inhale and straighten up to the starting position.

2. Exhale and repeat the movement to the other side. After 24 repetitions alternating sides, work one then the other side for 16 repetitions each.

Eight LEG SCISSORS

Starting position: Lie on your back with your hands under your buttocks. Extend your legs straight up.

1. Open your legs out to the sides and close them into the starting position, keeping them straight. Inhale when you open, exhale when you close. Do 24 repetitions.

2. With your straight legs opened wide, make small circles in the air.

Nine TRUNK STRETCHES

Starting position: Lie on your back, your legs straight and your arms stretched to the sides.

1. Bring your right knee first to your chest . . .

2. then to the floor on the left side, keeping your right shoulder on the floor. Hold this stretch for 20 seconds, then reverse sides.

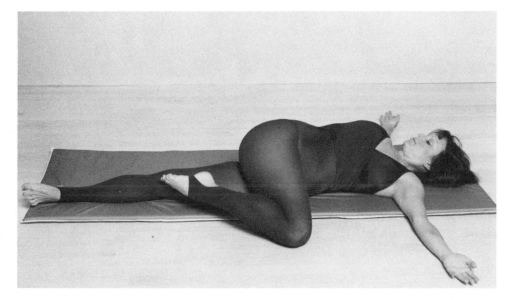

THE BUTTOCKS
One BUTTOCKS LIFTS

Starting position: Lie on your back with your arms alongside your body and your knees bent, your feet on the floor slightly more than hip distance apart.

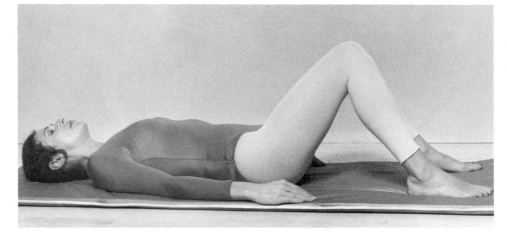

1. Keeping your shoulder blades on the floor, raise your buttocks. As you do, imagine that you are reaching with your lower back toward the floor. Now lift your buttocks slightly higher and release them down a little; lift, and release. This is a small movement done with the muscles underneath the buttocks. Exhale when you lift; inhale when you release. Repeat 24 times.

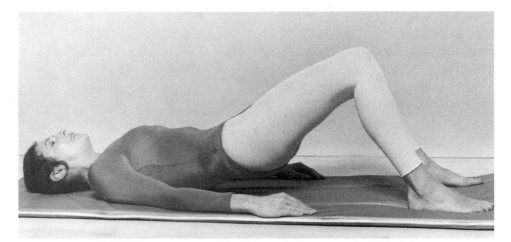

2. Walk your legs farther apart and continue the rhythmic lift-release of the buttock region. The movement is small. Your lower back presses toward the floor and your upper body does not move. Repeat 24 times.

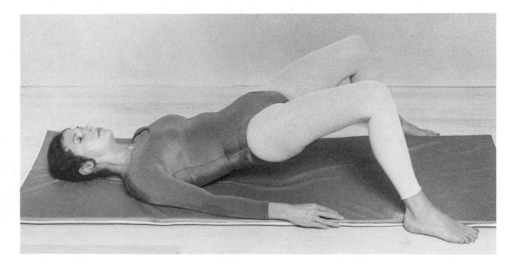

3. Now, without moving your feet or your upper body, bring your knees together and open them, all the time keeping your buttocks up.

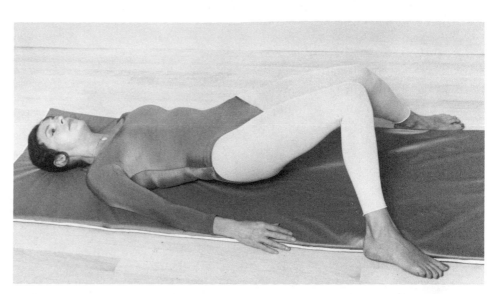

They'll move down slightly each time you open your knees and will come up again when you close them, but try to keep buttocks lifted. Open and close 24 times.

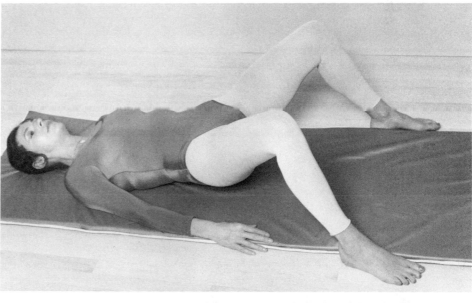

4. Walk your feet in a little closer together . . .

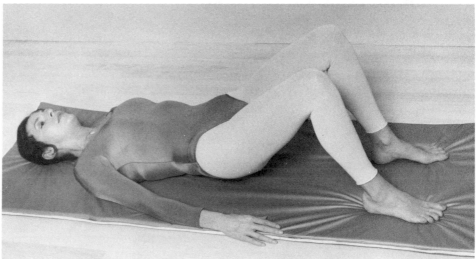

Continued ⟶

BUTTOCKS LIFTS (*continued*)

. . . and resume the rhythmic lift-release of the buttocks with your knees going in-out, in-out, in-out. The movement "out" takes care of itself, so you think "in, in, in, in, in." Repeat 24 times.

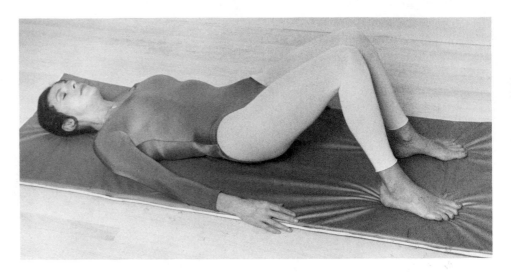

5. Walk your feet together and, with feet and knees touching, lift your buttocks up and release them slightly. Press up and release, press up and release. Your lower back is still pressing toward the floor and your upper body rests on the floor. Repeat 24 times.

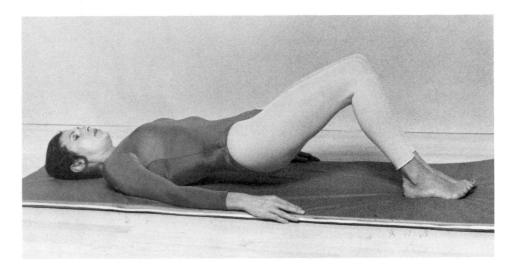

6. Now with your shoulder blades still on the floor, lift your buttocks up and hold them there, still pressing the lower back toward the floor. Feel the pelvis realign itself. Relax head, shoulders and arms. Hold for 20 to 30 seconds, then bring your buttocks down and straighten your legs.

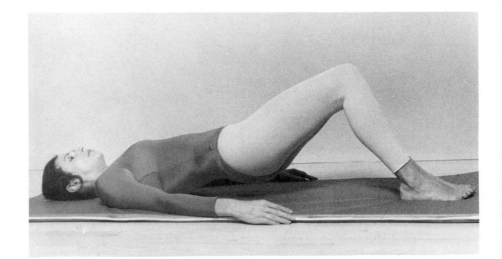

Two STRAIGHT LEG STRETCHES

Starting position: Lie on your back with your knees bent.

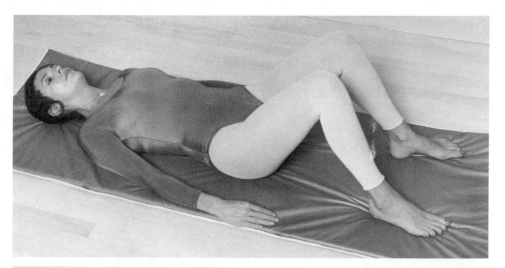

1. Bring your right knee to your chest; pull it closer.

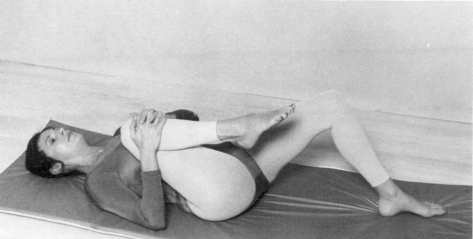

2. Straighten your leg and with your hands gently pull the straight leg as close to your body as possible.

Hold this stretch for 20 to 30 seconds, then put your right leg down and stretch your left leg the same way. Press your buttocks into the floor during this stretch.

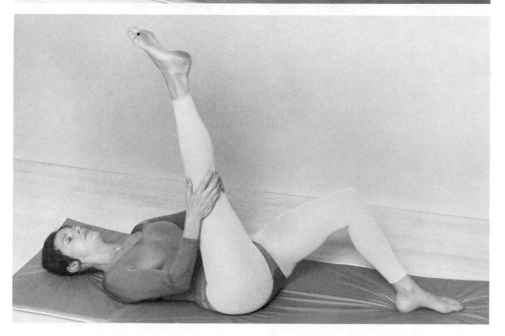

Three LOTUS LEANS

Starting position: Sit in a semi-lotus position.

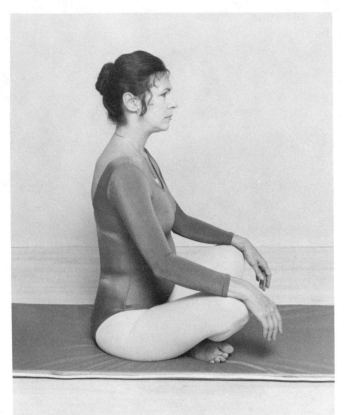

Lean straight forward over your legs and relax there. The buttock of your top leg will take most of the stretch, so change legs after 20 seconds to stretch the other side.

THE THIGHS
One CAT KNEE LIFTS

Starting position: Kneel on all fours and rock your pelvis in the cat-pose fashion a few times: Exhale, drop head and buttocks under and round the back up like an angry cat. Inhale and flatten the back. Then, with a flat back, balance your weight well between arms and legs.

1. Lift your right knee to the side, keeping your knee higher than your foot, and bring it down . . .

2. then lift this leg with a *bent* knee toward the back and bring it down.

After 24 repetitions alternating directions, do 24 lifts to the side, then 24 lifts to the back. During the 24 lifts to either direction, your leg does not come back to touch the floor but stays up, and you lift it up farther in small movements up, up, up. Rest a few moments, then repeat with the other leg.

Two CAT LEG LIFTS

Starting position: Distribute your weight evenly on your elbows and knees.

1. Bring your right knee to your chest . . .

2. then stretch your leg up and away to the back. Repeat 24 times, rest a few moments, then repeat with the other leg.

Three BUTTOCKS RELEASE

Starting position: Sit back on your legs with your buttocks close to your heels.

Lie forward with your chest on your knees and your face on the floor or mat. Stretch your arms forward past your head and stretch your buttocks closer to your heels. Relax into the stretch for 20 seconds.

WHEN YOU CAN DO THESE EXERCISES WITHOUT SORENESS, YOU ARE READY TO MOVE ON TO THE BEGINNING CLASS IN JANE FONDA'S WORKOUT BOOK.

Part Seven

Mothering an Infant

UNDERSTANDING YOUR BABY'S LANGUAGE

As adults, we crave variety, and consider monotony a terrible punishment. But we fear change if it means completely letting go of what we are used to, and during a period of transition we prefer to hang on to a few comfortable habits. Why would an infant be any different? In the womb the baby was rocked every time the mother moved, could drink when it pleased and was warm and cozy without effort on its part. So if you put it in a crib and keep it on a feeding schedule it will probably protest. I think the baby should be allowed to keep some of the comforts it had before it was born. Being held and allowed to nurse on demand while mastering the tasks of digestion, of staying warm and of relaxing into sleep and sleeping deeper for longer periods of time will not keep a baby from learning to entertain itself or to explore its environment. The first three months of life *are* the fourth trimester. Your arms and breasts have now taken the place of your uterus and placenta; and during this fourth trimester the baby should be weaned slowly from complete dependency to less frequent interaction.

An infant's gaze will touch your heart, its sweet smell is pleasing, and its soft cuddly body is a pleasure to hold. But its cry is more upsetting than anything you may ever have to listen to, and no one can bear it for long.

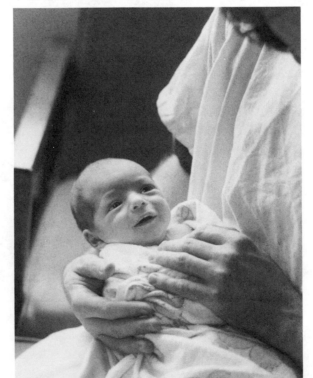

Perhaps a baby sitter would be able to turn up the music and close the nursery door, but most parents will feel compelled to try to find the cause of the crying. Unfortunately your baby can't tell you what is bothering it, so communication between parents and infant relies on more than listening. A mother develops such a fine sense of observing, reflecting, and reaching conclusions, in a way that so sharpens her awareness of others, that women are thought to have a sense which men lack. But men develop it in just the same way and an infant does not discriminate between its mother and father if the father cares for the child often.

The baby will cry for any number of reasons—it may be hungry, have gas pains, be too warm or too cold, need its diaper changed; it may be lying in an uncomfortable position, or it may want to be held. How can you tell which is which when the baby is new and you have never cared for an infant before? By holding it, by watching and, when it shows unhappiness through crying, straining, squirming or grimacing, by testing which remedy seems to make it more comfortable.

ITS PHYSICAL CHANGES

A baby's skin is velvety soft and more sensitive than we can imagine. Skin and nervous system evolve from the same layer of cells. Until birth the only exposure was to the fluid and soft lining of the mother's body. Stroke your baby gently with a relaxed hand, let the strokes flow away from the heart rather than toward it and your infant would probably purr if it could. But don't let it get too cool during bath or massage because then it will kick and cry in protest and to raise its temperature.

Rashes with little pimples are considered normal by pediatricians today. The first time a baby breaks out, on its cheeks or under the chin, you will wonder what you did to cause it; no one knows. If it does not seem to bother the baby, try not to pay attention to it and it will go away. Birthmarks, pinkish spots which become red when the baby cries, are quite common too. They fade during the first six months of life.

Until recently about half of all babies born—usually girls—were considered inferior because of their sex and were therefore often less welcome than the preferred sex. Today there is no justification for such a prejudice, and you can hope for a boy or a girl purely because you would like the experience of helping one or the other grow up.

Both boys and girls are at birth still influenced by the hormone levels of the pregnant mother. This commonly leads to swollen breasts—occasionally even with some mild secretion, to a rather full scrotum in boys, or occasionally to the discharge of a few drops of blood from a girl's vagina.

Our organs of reproduction are as sensitive at birth as they are through life. They do not need improvement. Any correction causes trauma and pain. In the most common one, circumcision, the skin which normally

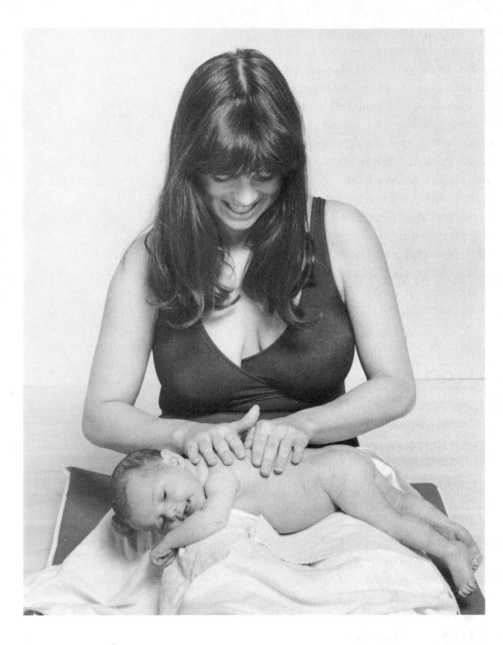

protects the sensitive tip of the penis is cut away. This operation is done routinely on Jewish boys as a religious ritual on the eighth day after birth. For non-Jewish babies it is done the first or second day. Most American pediatricians agree that there is no medical reason for this operation, and they have moved away from inflicting this trauma right after birth since the child already has so many adjustments to make. And there might be a physiological advantage to waiting. The blood-clotting mechanism becomes more mature and the parents get time to reflect and decide. But regardless of when the circumcision is done, it is still painful for the baby.

Care of a circumcised penis is simple and it heals fast. The small piece of vaselined gauze wrapped around the wound should be changed regularly, and the diaper should be put on so as to avoid its rubbing the wound as the baby moves. Mohels have quite an elaborate technique of wrapping penis and legs to prevent kicking and rubbing against the fresh wound.

On the second or third day after birth, the baby's skin may take on a yellowish tint. As part of the adjustment to extra-uterine life, the makeup of the blood changes. Inside the uterus the baby's need for oxygen-carrying red blood corpuscles was higher than it is after birth. The extra cells are broken down and the waste is processed by the liver. But this organ, the center of all metabolic activity, may not be able to keep up. If some of the waste remains in the circulation in a semi-broken-down state, a ski-tan color results.

Most babies get a little of it for a few days and it usually does not require treatment. Fluids help the breakdown of this bilirubin. Therefore let a somewhat jaundiced baby nurse as often as it likes. Offer at each feeding one, then the other breast, but only for a few minutes to make sure the baby does not waste suckling energy on an empty breast. Then offer it water through a bottle. Alternate the first breast at each feeding.

Jaundice is a cause for concern if the skin turns more rather than less yellow and if the baby sleeps more. If a bilirubin count, taken from a blood sample, is high for a baby's weight and maturity the liver can be stimulated to speed up the breakdown by exposing the baby to light. Since sunlight would cause sunburn, a special light has been devised. While the baby is under it, its eyes need to be covered and it should be undressed. It is customary today to make this exposure continuous except for brief interruption during nursing. But there is now good evidence that intermittent exposure works just as well for the liver and much more conveniently for parents and baby.

Since accumulation of bilirubin is sometimes a first warning of the onset of a more serious illness and occasionally the symptom of a discrepancy in blood between mother and baby, pediatricians advise that every baby with neonatal jaundice should be under medical supervision. This is especially important since it has recently been discovered that high levels of bilirubin can damage brain cells. Some doctors overreact, I think, to a slightly jaundiced baby, and send every one under the light. To my mind such an overreaction serves only the light factories and the hospital employees. Treatment should be reserved to cure harmful conditions; it is not a preventive measure. Prevention is done through proper health care and careful observation.

PHYSICAL CARE

Bacteria prey on us continuously and most of us carry our own stock around, which don't harm us because we have built up a defense against them. The baby gets this defense with its mother's milk. Therefore your house does not need to be sterilized. You merely need to prevent these bacteria from accumulating and taking over. Keep yourself and the baby clean, well rested and well nourished. In your home keep the bathroom clean, as well as the kitchen, your bed, and the baby's bed.

For some time after the delivery your resistance to infection will be lower than usual and your baby will be quite vulnerable too, so avoid unselected exposure. The supermarket, the nursery school and the movie theater are out for a few weeks. So is the hospital, unless there is a medical reason for being there. At home avoid contact with your friends' small children since they frequently transmit infectious diseases. Wherever the skin is open, bacteria can gain an easy foothold. The baby's navel while it is healing is such an area. In the days following birth the cord slowly turns black, it becomes stiff, hangs on by a thread and finally falls off. Then the belly button dries. Physicians recommend that the area be kept clean and dry until it is healed. Therefore they say not to submerge the baby in water, rather give it sponge baths until the cord has fallen off and the belly button is dry. But some little babies love being submerged in water. If you do bathe yours, make sure that both tub and baby are clean. Dry the baby well and use the warm air from a hand-held hair dryer to dry the belly button afterwards.

While the navel is healing, keep the baby's diapers below its belly button to prevent the navel from getting soaked in urine. Babies wet all the time and they don't need to be changed every time they are a little wet, especially if they show no sign of discomfort. If the skin on the buttocks is extra sensitive you will notice its redness, and have to change the baby more often. Rinse the area with lukewarm water to wash away the remnants of urine and dry it well, especially in the creases. Powder and lotion

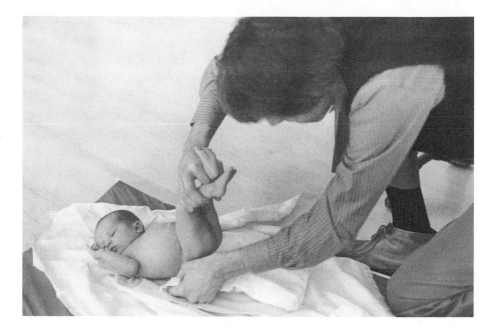

don't help the skin as much as water and a soft towel. The disposable wipes currently popular are fine for occasional use but they are harder on the skin than water. After a bowel movement, wash the area with extra care. If the stool was loose, make sure none of it remains around the foreskin or between the labia. With index finger and thumb, open the labia and, if necessary, wipe with a moist cotton ball. Always wipe away from, not toward, the vagina.

There does not need to be any regularity in the frequency, color or consistency of the bowel movements of a breast-fed infant. If a baby skips a day, it will strain a little more the next day. It will probably prefer to make this effort while at the breast.

A small baby does not really need a changing table. It is quite as easily changed on your lap or next to you on the bed. A small foam pad covered with plastic and a towel laid over the sink in your bathroom may work well too, especially since you have running water handy there. Do not leave your baby unattended in such a place for even an instant because infants practice new skills such as rolling over from a very early age. Infants tend to fuss more during a diaper change when they are flat on their back on a firm surface than when they are allowed a more cuddly position on a more inviting surface.

A baby's nose, ears and eyes do not need cleaning on a regular basis. If there is a lot of mucus in the nose, this is easiest removed with a suction bulb. Do it carefully and only when necessary. Indent the bulb slightly. Insert it into the nose so the tip is not against the membrane. Release the indentation and the resulting suction will pick up the mucus. Mucus in the eye can be gently wiped away with a sterile Q-tip. Mothers have observed that a few drops of mother's milk carefully placed in the corner of the eye near the nose often clears up a beginning eye infection. If it does

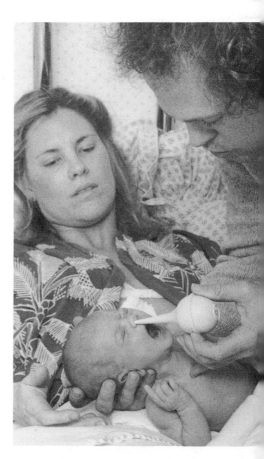

not and the secretion of mucus continues or especially if it increases, medical attention is a must.

If you give your baby a sponge bath, undress it from the waist up. Wash it, rinse it and dry it with special attention to those areas where the skin folds on itself: behind the ears, at the neck, under the arms, and with a fat little baby, at the elbows. Some mothers like to make sure those areas are dry by putting a little cornstarch on their fingers and sliding the powdered fingers over the skin. Too much cornstarch will form a crust and increase chances that the skin underneath gets irritated. Don't shake it on so it makes clouds of dust which your baby will breathe. Then dress the baby's top half, undress and wash the lower half and dry it, again giving special attention to the creases in the skin.

When the time has come for a tub bath, the baby will still experience cooling as a distress. Therefore have a pre-warmed towel and clean clothes and the bath water ready before you undress your baby. Work quickly: undress the baby, soap it with a wet wash cloth or your hands, and test the temperature of the water with your elbow. If it feels pleasantly warm pick up your wet and slippery baby in such a manner that it cannot fall, and lower it into the tub to rinse it off. Lift it out of the water into a warm dry towel, then dress it at your leisure if you are both having a nice time. Many parents take their baby into the tub with them when they take a bath. Babies seem to enjoy such a shared bath quite a bit. But do wait to do this until its navel has healed.

In cool weather the baby will be more comfortable in an outfit which covers arms, legs and feet. Babies don't like to have their hands covered. Their fingers and fists are their first toys. Just keep the nails short and the scratches your baby inadvertently gives itself will remain very minor. On a warm day, when your baby is awake and kicking, an undershirt and diaper or nothing at all may be fine. But when it is asleep it will almost always need a cover to remain comfortably warm.

HELPING YOUR BABY WITH GROWING PAINS

The cycles of deep and light sleep alternate at short intervals in an infant. When it sleeps close to you and you see it start to move about but you know it could not yet be hungry, rock it gently or place a hand on its behind and pat it a little to help it ease into another cycle of deeper sleep. Infants intuitively look for the presence of the mother's body for care and nourishment whenever they surface out of deep sleep.

Air which did not come up right after nursing will often cause trouble five to ten minutes later. To help your baby burp, hold it up against your body with its head so supported that it cannot drop back. Or set your

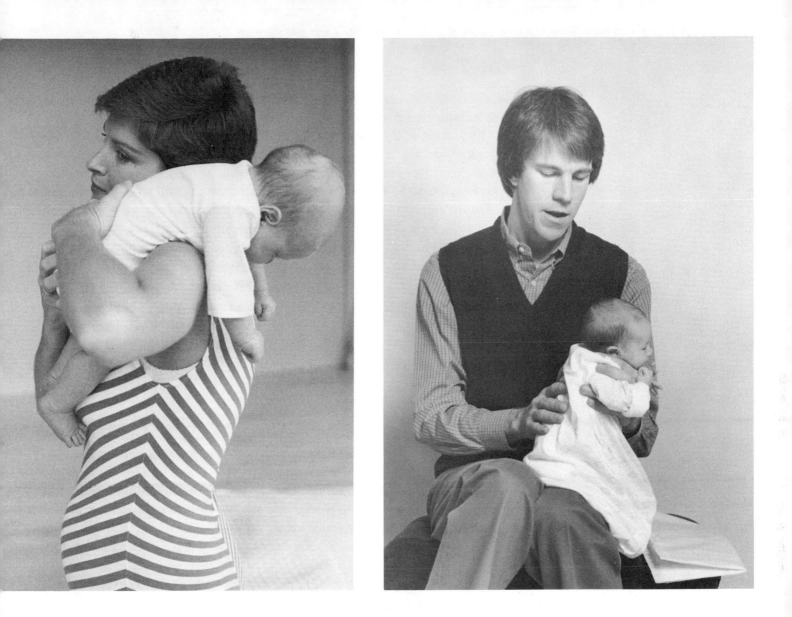

baby on your knee. Notice that an infant is not able to sit erect by its own strength. When you let it sag, the air will not come up as easily as when you support it upright. Place the palm of one wide-open hand against your baby's chest and let your index finger and thumb support its head at the chin. Let your baby lean slightly forward with its chest in your hand. Place your other hand against its lower back and waist area for support. If the burp does not come, rock it back and forth a few times. Its behind remains on your knee while you swing the upper body with good support gently back then forward. After a few movements, hold it upright again and while still supporting it at the chest, let the other hand gently pat the area behind the stomach and make little strokes up-up-up from the lower back to the shoulder blades.

If crying starts twenty minutes or so after a feeding, the bowels are probably hurting. Gentle warm pressure may well relieve the worst of it, especially if you combine pressure with the diversion of rocking. Place the baby with its belly on the rounding of your shoulder. Let its buttocks sit in your cupped hand so your index finger and thumb fit in the slight indentation there. This relaxes the muscles along the baby's spine. Let your other hand caress the area from the lower back to the waist. Your baby's head and arms will hang over your shoulders. Let it settle in cozily by bringing your head close to its little head. The baby's body weight provides the pressure and your shoulder the warmth. Your rocking or walking gives it a desired diversion and maybe the crying will stop. But when a new cramp comes the crying may start again. Just talk to your baby and rock it and rub it. You will feel its legs draw up and its body tighten, and when the cramp is over, the baby relaxes to doze off to sleep. After ten to fifteen minutes, the worst of the cramps is probably over.

If the baby falls asleep and your shoulder needs a rest, try putting it down, but remember that it was warmth, pressure, movement and your presence that helped it fall asleep. Don't take all of these away at the same time. Prewarm the spot where you are planning to put your baby with a hot-water bottle, filled less than one-third with water that is *warm,* not hot. Remove the air by pressing the sides of the bottle together above the water and close the bottle carefully while the sides are still together. Put this hot-water bottle over a diaper roll, cover the rubber with a diaper or a receiving blanket, and on top of everything place a soft cuddly blanket. Open the blanket when it feels warmed, put the baby on its belly on top of the rolled-up diaper and hot-water bottle, and drape the warmed blanket gently around the baby. Place your hand on its behind and rock it very gently, talking softly to it as you work. When the baby settles in and stays asleep, you can walk away proud and pleased.

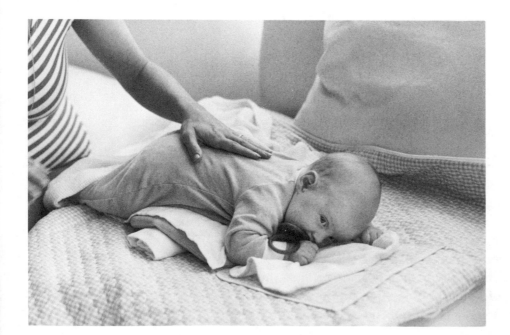

Infants grow from minute to minute. These continuous achievements will show in leaps and bounds. Every aspect of growth places an immediate new challenge on the busy system, sometimes causing the baby a temporary distress. Thus when an infant sheds some of its newborn quality, when its gaze becomes more focused, its muscle tone stronger and its ability to ask for attention more pronounced, it may also need to eat more often and be more bothered by cramps. Many mothers notice this change between five days and two weeks. Don't get frightened when your so-called "good" baby is suddenly more demanding. A really "good" baby is the one able to ask for what it needs, because that shows a healthy development.

Allow the baby to nurse as often as it needs to. But don't misuse the breast. Don't force it on the baby as the solution to all its problems. Sharpen your skills of observation and drawing conclusions and put these to the test. Intuition is an ability each parent needs to develop in order to respond to a particular child instead of to a generality drawn about children.

When your baby cries and neither food nor diaper or position change ease the distress, assume that its bowels are giving it painful contractions. Now recollect what you learned about pain during labor. Fear made it worse. Yet every time a strong contraction came on, fear did arise. When you looked at a trusted face and that face showed calm caring, your fear lessened and you could let your body work. It was still painful but not quite as frightening and lonely. If a hand touched you in the right spot, that too made it better. And, while kisses were nice when a contraction was over, in the middle of one they would have been quite out of place. Apply these insights to helping your baby. With one major difference: your baby perceives the feelings of others more directly than you did during labor. Therefore you have to overcome your responses of fear and panic when your baby cries so desperately because they will intensify its innate response to pain—tension and irregular breathing. Your baby is little, vulnerable, and sensitive. You are big and strong. You say, "Oh my little baby, I know you are hurting, but nothing is seriously wrong. It is just your bowels, from all your eating and growing. Let me try to help you with it. We'll work on it together."

Place your baby face up on your legs with its head toward your knees and its legs folded against your belly. This bending up of its legs relaxes the abdominal muscles. Offer the baby a pacifier or just the nipple from a water bottle plugged with a cotton ball. Encourage your baby to suck on it because such sucking relaxes the gut without putting anything in the stomach. Sometimes it helps to move the pacifier slightly in and out of its mouth to help it realize that this is very different from the breast. Place a warm hand—if your hands are not warm, rub them together until they are—on your baby's belly. Allow this hand to relax, let the weight of the warm hand go into its belly, then slowly encompass it a little more firmly

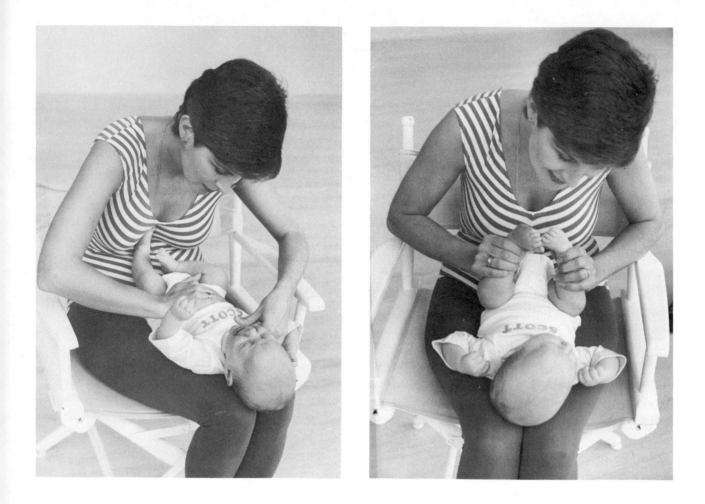

so you feel that its belly is contained by your hand. With your other hand gently knead the top of its shoulders, touch its chest and arms. During a strong cramp you will feel your baby tighten all its muscles, and its belly may get hard. Keep it cupped protectively in your hand. When the cramp and the crying cease, take your baby's legs in your hands. Rotate them gently in the hips by bringing the knees close to the belly and away, close and away. Then press both knees gently on the belly, hold them there a few moments, let go, take the legs by the ankles and stretch them up along the baby's body, reaching its toes toward its chin. The baby will probably release some gas. If not, stroke the belly in a rhythmic fashion from just below the bottom edge of the ribcage to the pubic area. Place the side of one hand right at the bottom edge of the rib cage. Slide it down to the top of the legs while the other hand is placed at the edge of the rib cage. After a few rhythmic strokes, cup the belly with one hand, place the thumb of your other hand (covered with a Kleenex, if you like) on the baby's rectum, and press here very slightly. The baby will respond by straining and, let's hope, will expel some gas. If another cramp comes along with a more vigorous crying spell and you feel that holding the belly

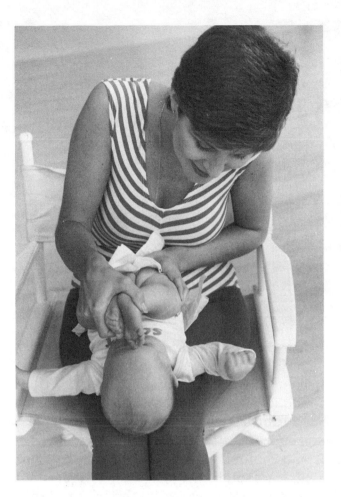

and rubbing the shoulders did not help very much, try the position where the belly leans on your rounded shoulder. In this position most babies prefer to be walked rather than rocked. If neither one of these positions brings much relief, fill a rubber hot-water bottle so it is flat, like a waterbed, and radiates a pleasant warmth. Place this bottle on your leg and let your baby rest on it with its belly. Rock, talk and caress the baby so it knows you are there to help and that the pain is not serious and will go away. When the baby eases into sleep you might be able to put it in its own bed for a while. If it has been a difficult day, put it on the hot-water bottle, but make sure that this does not leak and that the water in it is *warm,* not hot!

After a serious attack of cramps, some babies need to nurse again. Don't be reluctant. You can't let your baby go without nursing for fear that it will bring on new cramps. Maybe it won't. And if it does, reevaluate your diet. Try leaving out dairy products for a week to ten days. If that makes no difference, try something else. Some nursing mothers discover that a lot of raw vegetables in their diet make a baby's cramps worse. Others say that the cramps eased when they took yeast twice a day or in

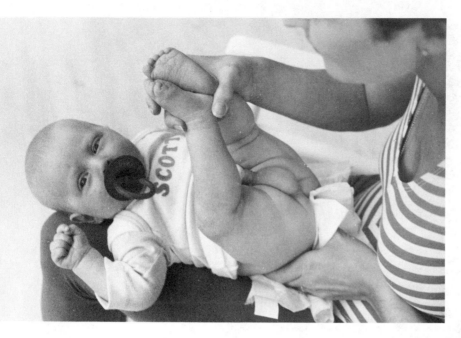

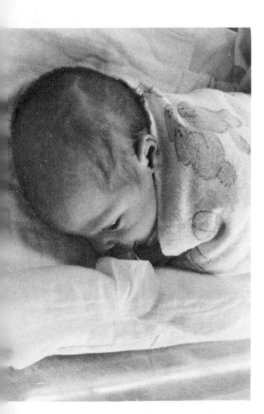

some other way improved their diet. Also consider offering your baby chamomile tea some of the time instead of water between feeding because chamomile tea sometimes releases stomach cramps.

Some babies can stay comfortable only when they have something to suck on. A pacifier is fine but a baby loses it easily and fusses every time the pacifier drops out of its mouth. Take the screw top and nipple off a bottle. Plug the nipple well with cotton then cut a piece of cardboard to fill the screw top. Now tape this contraption at a right angle to a rolled-up diaper. The busy nurses in intensive-care nurseries use this trick and thus avoid a lot of extra trips to help babies find lost pacifiers.

If your baby has a few days of constant fussing occasionally interrupted only by a brief nap, you will become tense and begin to feel inadequate and resentful. There is nothing more confusing and painful than not being able to help your child. But you are helping it by being there. As a parent you cannot always take your baby's pain away, nor can you prevent traumas of another nature. Your task is to help your child deal with what occurs while you try to protect it from what it cannot yet handle.

SPECIAL PROBLEMS

If your baby was born with a special problem, your love and ability to help it develop those parts which function well will be invaluable. None of us is perfect, but we all have the ability to compensate. Those who cannot learn to be long-distance runners may cover more miles with their minds. Those whose minds are not capable of deep thought and reflection may arouse our love by their sweet natures. A baby who was born so prematurely that it cannot be held and cuddled the way you would like does not miss this as much as you do. Touch it and hold it as much as its condition allows, and with your love it will grow into a trusting and cheerful child in spite of the fact that it was technology more than your care which helped it live those first weeks.

Some babies are born so perceptive and so impatient to get going that they cannot process all they take in. Their nervous systems become over-stimulated, resulting in irritable tension in every muscle cell. Such babies cry frequently or continuously during the period from one week to three or four months, and occasionally longer. During rare moments when the baby feels well, its parents get a glimpse of the delightful character of their offspring, but most of the time the little person is impossible to be with. Do what you can. Don't feel guilty. Don't worry about your baby's psyche. When the bodily discomfort ceases, your baby's behavior will not reveal any remnants of its hard times. Such babies are not necessarily helped by rest and quiet. Especially during a crying spell they seem to prefer motion. A ride in a stroller, a drive in the car, rocking and walking, being danced to music are among the techniques women report as helpful. And more helpful still is to let someone else take over for a while—some-one not worn out by days of hovering over a crying baby. Call on your friends, your relatives, and on your partner. Often fathers can ease a baby's irritable cry better than mothers because they do not get quite as pulled into the baby's distress and they do not smell like milk, thus con-fusing the baby as to what it wants or needs.

If no help is available and you feel torn between wanting to help and not having any time for yourself, put the baby down when you know it is not hungry, wet, cold, or being stuck by a diaper pin and talk to it: "I have had it with you. I want to brush my teeth and my hair, have some coffee and read the newspaper. And you are going to try to go to sleep. If you can't, you may cry but it will be a little while before I can carry you again." Return to your baby when you have resolved the tension between your need to help it and your need to take care of yourself, and then you will feel more like being with your baby again.

INTRODUCING ACTIVITIES

When you begin to move about more, take your baby with you on walks in your arms or held up against your chest—first in your house where you describe your favorite places, then outside in your garden or in your neighborhood. Walking is an excellent exercise, especially when you take care to walk as if you were carrying a basket on your head. With the crown of your head thus extended, your posture improves and your walk-ing will exercise every muscle without causing strain. When you sit with your baby on your lap, gently rock it and stroke it while you read, talk with friends, watch TV, or listen to music.

Once your baby is strong enough to be carried in a sling, your hands are free again. Such a sling must have been one of woman's earliest inventions. It may have come closely after the digging stick. Your baby will like being in it while you straighten up your home and do your shopping more than when you sit down to read. During reading it is easier to rock the baby on your lap.

Some mothers regularly give their babies a sun bath. Start with one minute on each side and protect the skull and the eyes. Increase the amount by a half a minute each time and soon your baby will have a lovely suntan all over. Sunlight helps diaper rash. So does exposure to air. But don't put a bare-skinned infant who is not used to sun directly in that light for more than a minute.

BABY MASSAGE

People in India, whether rich or poor, massage their babies regularly. A restaurant owner in Los Angeles told me how his father used mustard oil and after the massage rolled him in the warm sand.

A very small baby will often tolerate only a few strokes, but at about four weeks a baby begins to enjoy a full massage; at the right moment, that is. After a massage, even after one which involved only a few strokes, a baby under three to four months usually needs to suckle. It will cry from misunderstanding and impatience if you insist on dressing it first. So just quickly close the diaper, wrap it up in a towel and put it to the breast, or give it the bottle. An older baby will enjoy exercises and a bath after a massage.

Most strokes are done from the heart outward and always only with the weight of a relaxed hand; never use pressure. Your first strokes should aim to release tension. Remember what you learned when you were having a massage: the thoughtful attention of the other person combined with his skillful hands are what make it delightful. Rhythm and careful completion of each stroke add to the pleasure too. When you work on a leg, work on the leg. But be aware that the legs start right at the body and not in the middle of the thighs, so to work on the legs you have to undo the baby's diaper. Keep it handy to catch an unexpected present.

I don't believe that sequence of parts is very important. I am inclined to start with the back, then do the chest, next the arms and hands, the legs and feet, then the belly, and finally the face. The back is done most easily when the baby lies face down and crosswise over one's legs. First loosen

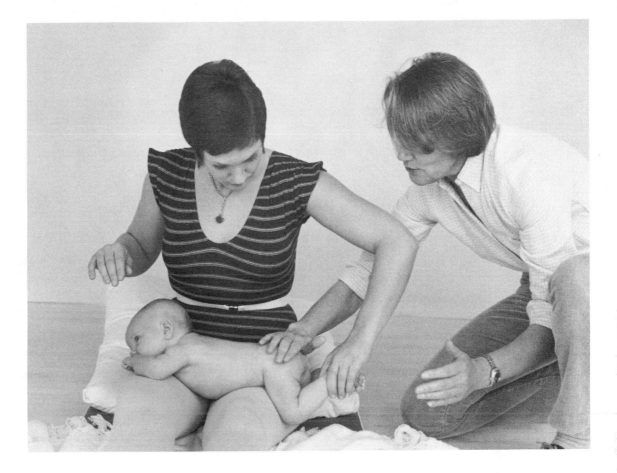

the baby's muscles by sliding your hands side to side across its back starting at the neck and working down to the buttocks. Then cup the hand
closest to the buttocks around these two little hills in a caressing supportive fashion and slide the other hand rhythmically down the spine from the
neck to where it meets the hand on the buttocks. After some strokes, slide
the hand on the buttocks down the legs to grasp the ankles. Now make
rhythmic strokes all the way from the neck down to the back, over the
buttocks and the back of the legs to the hand on the feet. If your hand
does not slide smoothly, rub it with one or two drops of a non-perfumed
oil.

If you and your baby enjoyed this, maybe you can try the chest. Turn
your baby over and place it on your legs, or between your open legs on a
towel, or on a soft pad on a table in front of you. Position yourself so that
you will not get tense and fatigued. Tell your baby that you'll stop when it
tells you it's had enough. Place your hands on your baby's chest letting
the index fingers meet in the middle of the chest without touching the
belly. Now stroke outward with the motion you would make if you were
pressing open a precious book with a fine binding. A few rhythmic strokes,
then rest one hand cupped around the shoulder while you move the other

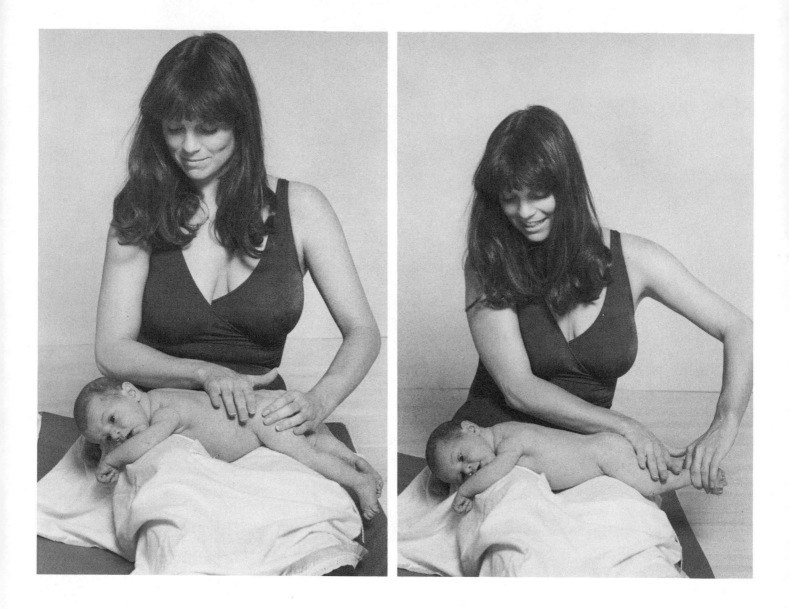

to the baby's opposite flank. Move the hands rhythmically and diagonally across the chest; hip to shoulder, shoulder to hip.

The arms are easier to stroke when you turn your baby slightly on its side. First make a long stroke with both your hands around the baby's arm from the top of the shoulder to the wrist. Then place both hands at the base of its arm and move them slowly and in opposite directions down to its wrist. Next make a few light long strokes again from the top of the arm to the wrist. Take the baby's hand (or fist), and make a few gentle rotations with your fingertips on the top of its wrist, then gently stroke that hand open. Stroke, do not pry. If your baby's fist is clenched, leave it closed. It may take a while before your baby gains control over opening and closing its hand.

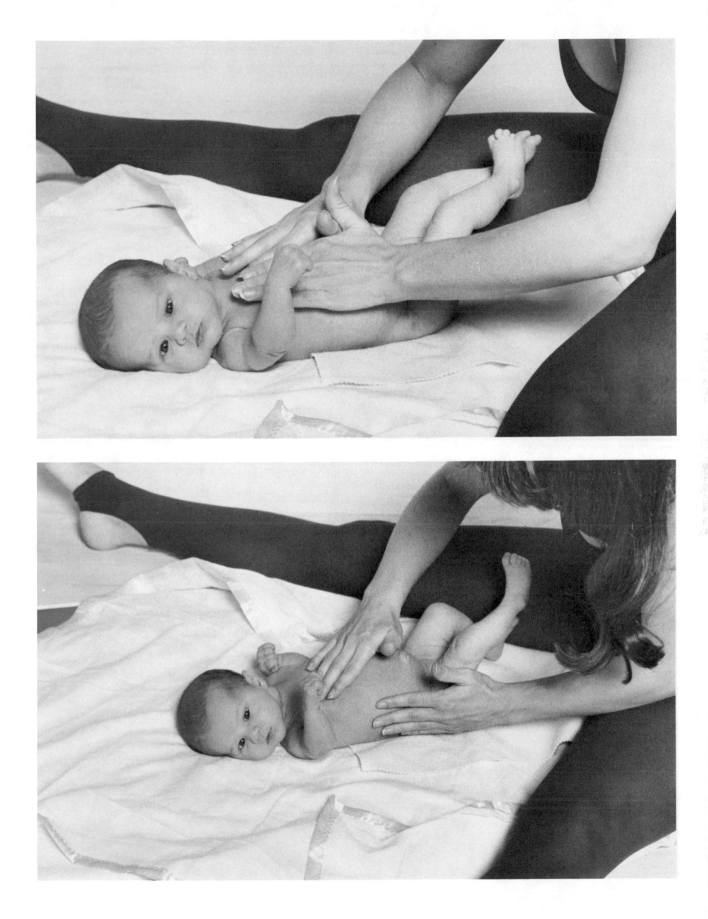

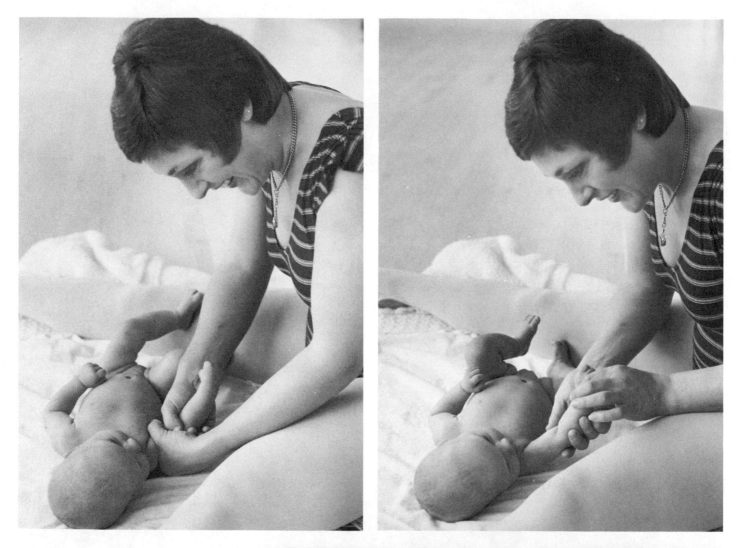

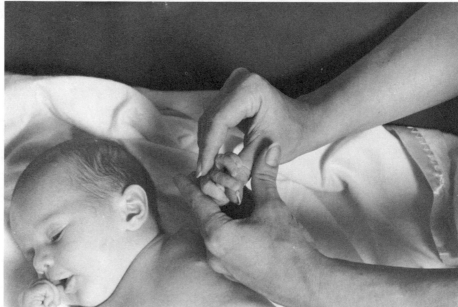

The legs are next. First give one leg a long stroke with both hands all the way from the top of the thigh to the ankle. Then place both hands next to each other way up around the inner thigh. Now move them down the leg while twisting them slightly in opposite directions. Repeat the same movement once more from the thigh on down. Then with light strokes, slide one hand after the other down the leg from its joint at the hip to the ankle. Next take the little foot in your hand and make a few small rotations with the fingertips on the top of the foot. Then stroke the sole with your thumbs from the heel to the toes or stroke it with the palm of your hands, but be careful to use enough pressure so that you don't tickle the foot. Do the same with the other leg.

Now look at your baby's belly. The belly is a very sensitive part; the organs are not protected by bones here and they take on much of the tensions of living. If your hands are not warm, rub them together vigorously, then place one on the belly. Let it rest there and let the warmth of your hand radiate into and mix with the warmth of the baby's belly. Then in a rhythmic fashion, stroke the belly from the bottom of the rib cage to the pubic bone with alternate hands.

To complete the massage stroke your baby's forehead and temples and other parts of its face the way you know it likes to be caressed. But if the baby was ready to nurse before you have completed the massage, just put it to the breast.

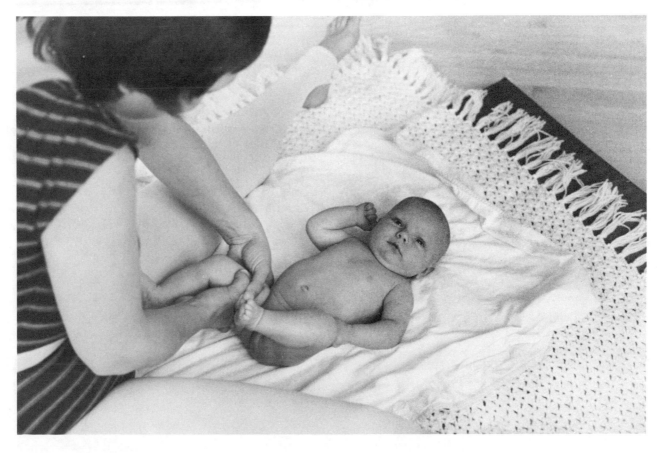

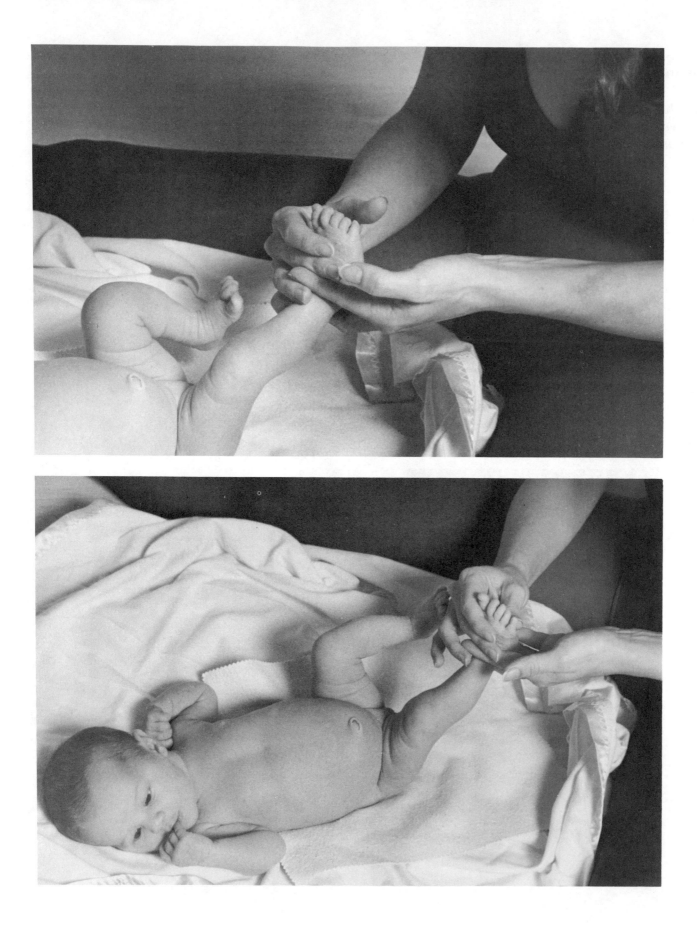

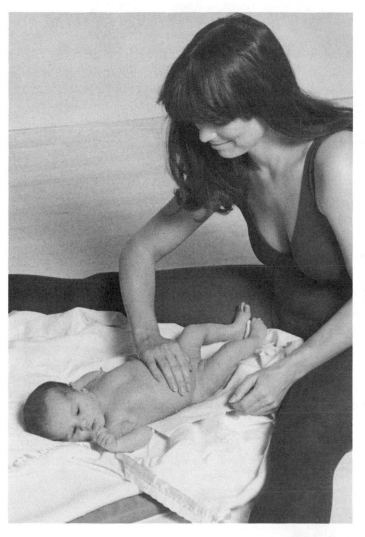

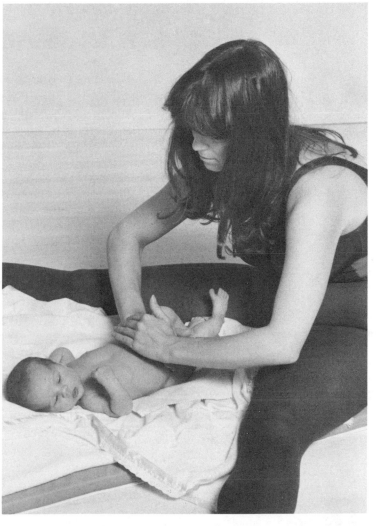

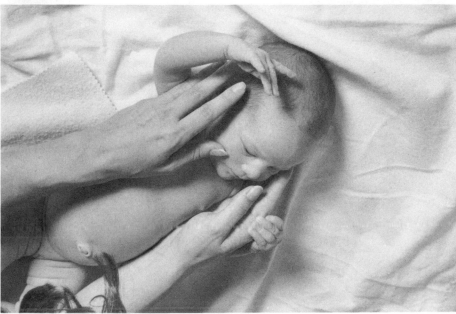

EXPANDING YOUR OWN AND YOUR BABY'S HORIZONS

After the period following childbirth when you need rest and privacy, you will want to meet with others again. Your baby may be ready for more variety too. It probably likes your arms, the sling, its bed, your bed, a rocker, a swing, a car ride and the stroller. But above all it likes pleasant company. Therefore if being home with your baby is beginning to bore you, your baby won't be too happy either. Go to the store, join a class where infants are welcome or visit a friend. Just go, don't wait until everything is under control and organized—it probably won't be that way for a few months. Don't be embarrassed—everyone who has taken care of an infant knows that the constant interruptions interfere with one's ability to keep order.

When your baby meets someone new, it will look to you to make sure that person is safe. While it may look freely and even smile at someone else while you hold it, in the other's arms it may well turn its head away, cry, or fall asleep if it isn't comfortable with the new person.

Most babies love being talked to. A baby talks back by moving its whole body. Some almost jump out of their infant seats when they get involved in a conversation. Next they'll move their lips. Then they will make sounds. They master the intonation of a sentence before they can articulate words. Mothers hear their babies repeat phrases like "all gone" and "bye-bye" long before those words are pronounced.

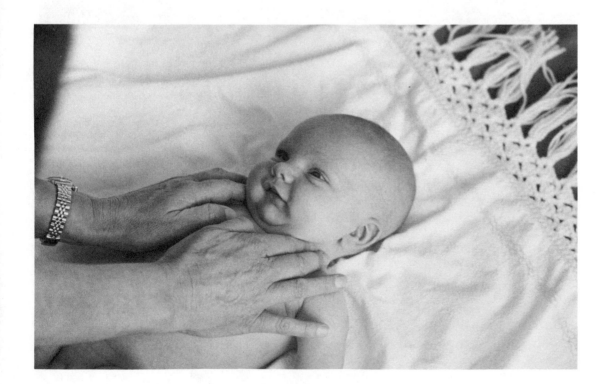

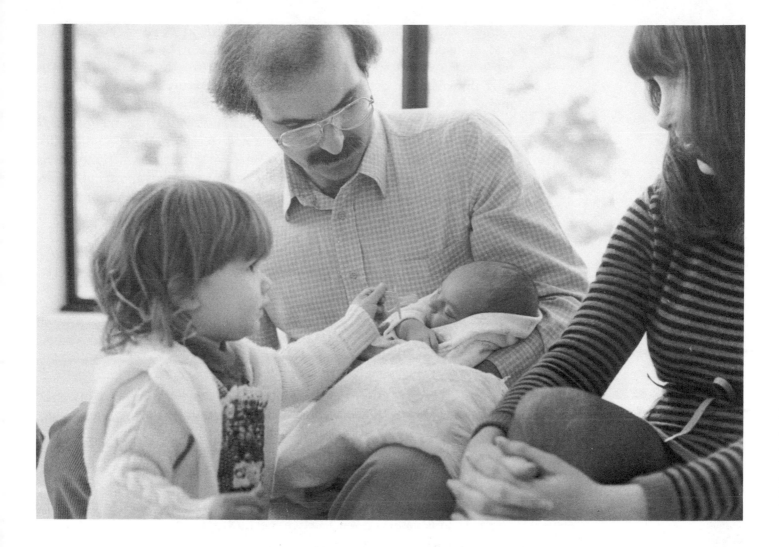

SETTING LIMITS

Babies are human yet they do lack one of our adult attributes: the ability to plot and plan. A baby does not cry with the thought, "If I cry, he'll come pick me up." It cries because it needs something. And it is the parent's task to determine what that something is and whether or not the baby should have it. A child will not be spoiled by your caring attention if you observe the following guide: encourage it to do for itself what it can, help it with what it cannot, and do not allow it to do what you truly disapprove of. Therefore do not let your child do something repeatedly which truly upsets you. Your resentment is much more confusing to him than your setting limits. While the initial days of mothering are ones of intense observation and of almost total giving, there comes a point where you must respond with a "no" to one of your baby's demands. For most women, the first limit is over play during the night. A baby should be fed and changed, helped with its pains and if it needs it, be allowed to sleep in one's arms, but it should not expect play at three in the morning. The next limit is often over eating at night. If your baby skips a feeding one night, don't be too quick to feed it at that time the next night. Should it wake up, rock it a little, give it some water and see if you can get it to go back to sleep. If not and the fussing changes to crying, or especially when the crying becomes desperate, feed it once more but be a little more reluctant to do so each night. With such encouragement most babies are able to give up night feedings somewhere between two weeks and three months. A general rule for helping a baby accomplish such growth is to watch for a sign that the baby is ready to make a change, then allow for the slight regression which often follows a growth spurt, but encourage it at the same time to accomplish what it was trying to do.

ASSUMING YOUR PLACE IN THE WORLD AS A MOTHER

Toward the end of the "fourth trimester," which, with an eye on individual variety, will last between two and four months, your baby may begin to leave you a little more time for yourself. Don't feel guilty if you want to return to work, school or some other activity outside the home. Motherhood was never intended to be a career. Women have always raised their children as well as running their households and a number of other things simultaneously. With our modern technology households are much easier to run, and it seems unrealistic to expect a woman to feel entirely fulfilled at home with her baby.

Also, a new mother finds herself more concerned about the course of the world, the quality of life in her community and the way other children are raised. So I think women's desire to return to some form of meaningful work is not a fad. Feminism and economic necessity are certainly contributing factors, but more important I think is the need of a mature human being to be a creative member of her community again.

Try not to feel pressured to return to work before you are ready, nor to stay home longer than feels right to you. Instead, pay attention to your interaction with your baby, assess the general circumstances of your life, then decide what is best for you. Parenthood starts at home as a very private relationship. But as the child matures and both of you venture out in the world, you will realize that caring for your child means caring about the world.

Index